Crocheting School

Crocheting School

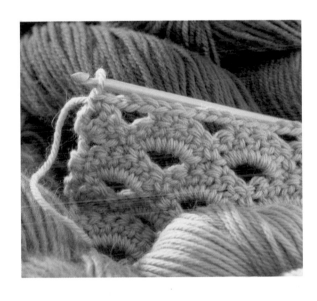

A Complete Course

Sterling Publishing Co., Inc.
New York

Translated by Mary Beth Benbenek

Published by Sterling Publishing Co., Inc.
387 Park Avenue South, New York, NY 10016
Originally published in Italy by RCS Libri SpA
under the title *Scuola di uncinetto*
© 2001 by RCS Libri SpA, Milano
English translation © 2004 by Sterling Publishing Co., Inc.
Distributed in Canada by Sterling Publishing
c/o Canadian Manda Group, One Atlantic Avenue, Suite 105
Toronto, Ontario, Canada M6K 3E7
Distributed in Great Britain by Chrysalis Books Group PLC
The Chrysalis Building, Bramley Road, London W10 6SP, England
Distributed in Australia by Capricorn Link (Australia) Pty. Ltd.
P.O. Box 704, Windsor, NSW 2756, Australia

ISBN 13: 978-1-4027-0831-2

Contents

What You Need

Tools

A **crochet hook** is the basic tool. It is simply a rod with a hook on the end:

- **Small (steel)**: For working with fine yarns and cotton threads. Numbers range from 14 (smallest) to 00.
- **Medium and Large (aluminum, plastic, or wood)**: For working thicker yarns. Sizes range alphabetically from B (2.25mm) to P (16mm).

Afghan (Tunisian) Hooks: These are longer than normal crochet hooks to accommodate the many stitches of afghan crocheting. Sizes are the same as for aluminum crochet hooks.

Hairpin Lace Tool: This is a U-shaped tool (like a giant hairpin) used for making special lace strips.

Other useful tools include: **yarn needles** for seams and finishing, rustproof **safety pins** for markers in your work, and **bobbins** for multicolored (jacquard) work.

Yarns

Linen, cotton, wool, silk, raffia, ribbon, strips of fabric or leather, string, or even thread can all be used for crocheting clothing or home furnishings.

For many yarns, the recommended hook size is indicated on the label. In general, the thicker the yarn, the larger the hook size needed. Thin or firmly twisted yarns are easier to work with, and show the pattern stitches better, than novelty yarns that are fuzzy or looped (bouclé).

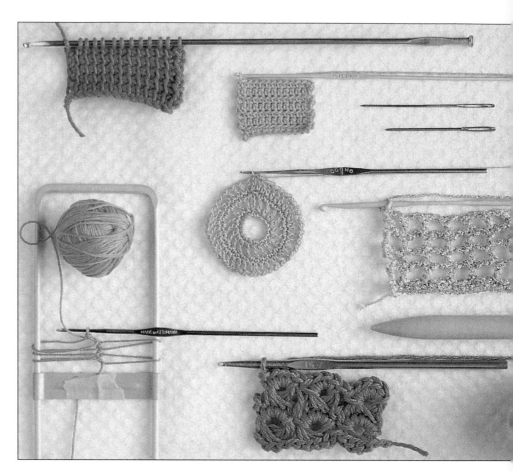

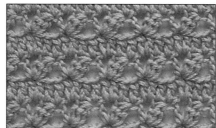

Knitting Worsted

Mohair Yarn

Fine Cotton

Medium Cotton

Heavy Cotton

Holding the Hook and Yarn

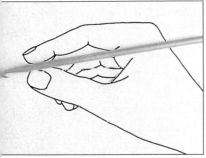

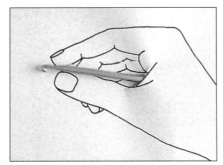

How to hold a crochet hook
Hold the crochet hook in your right hand, as if it were a pencil, and the yarn held in your left hand. If you are left-handed, hold the hook in your left hand and the yarn in your right. Your work will simply be the mirror image of what is shown.

How to hold an afghan hook
Grasp the afghan hook in your right (or left) hand as if you were holding a paring knife. Hold the yarn in the other hand. You can also grasp a crochet hook this way, if you prefer.

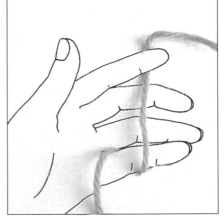

How to hold the yarn
Wrap the yarn around your little finger as shown. Pass it over your ring and middle finger, then behind and over your index finger.

How to hold the hairpin
Grasp the hairpin with the thumb and index finger of your left hand. Hold the crochet hook in your right hand as if it were a pencil.

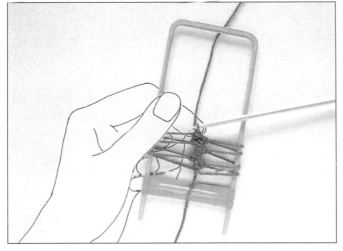

Sample Piece
Before starting any project, always work a sample piece first to be sure you are working the stitches to the correct gauge or size.

Make a gauge sample about 4 inches by 4 inches (10 cm x 10 cm), working in the desired stitch. With a tape measure, measure how many stitches across and how many rows you have per inch. If you have fewer stitches or rows than desired, use a smaller hook. If you have too many stitches or rows, use a larger hook.

2 inches (5 cm) of single crochet yields 10 stitches and 10 rows (5 sc and 5 rows =1").

2 inches (5 cm) of double crochet yields 10 stitches and 4 rows (5 dc and 2 rows =1").

How to Follow Directions

Abbreviations and Terms

beg = beginning
bl = block
ch = chain
cm = centimeter
dc = double crochet
dec = decrease
dtr = double treble
hdc = half double crochet
inc = increase
lp = loop(s)
rep = repeat
rnd = round
sc = single crochet
sk = skip
sl st = slip stitch
sp = space
st = stitch
sts =stitches
tog = together

tr = treble
tr tr = treble treble
yo = yarn over

* to * = Repeat instructions from first asterisk to second asterisk as many times as indicated.
( ) = Explanation of directions *or* series of steps between parentheses to be worked as indicated.
mark the stitch/row = Attach safety pin to work where indicated.
multiple = Number of stitches needed to work one repeat of pattern.
work even = Work without increasing or decreasing.

Easy or Difficult?

On many printed directions, you may find an indication of the difficulty of that particular project.

★ = easy

★★ = moderately difficult

★★★ = difficult

★★★★ = very difficult

Common Symbols Used for Diagram Directions

⇄ = direction of work

◠ = chain

● = slip stitch

△ = beginning of work

▲ = end of work

✕ = single crochet

⋎ = single crochet in relief

✖ = reverse single crochet

┬ = half double crochet

† = double crochet

‡ = treble

‡ = double treble

‡ = treble treble

ƒ = post double crochet around front

ƒ = post double crochet around back

= 3 double crochet cluster

= 5 double crochet cluster

= 5 double crochet popcorn

= 5 double crochet shell

= 2 crossed double crochet

= 2 crossed double crochet with chain

= decrease in double crochet

= 2 stitch decrease in double crochet

= 4 stitch decrease in double crochet

= picot

= 5-chain arch

= 3-chain arch

= joining bar

8

How to Begin
Simple Chain (ch)

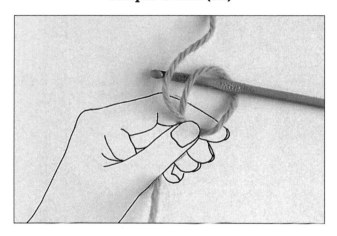

1 Holding the yarn end in your left hand, form a loop as shown. With your right hand, insert the hook through the loop and catch the yarn with the hook.

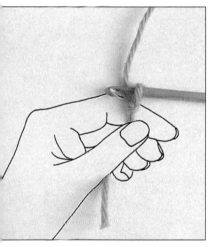

2 Draw the yarn on the hook through the loop and pull the yarn end with your left hand to tighten the stitch on the hook.

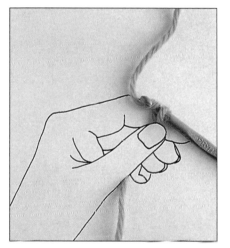

3 Holding the base of the first chain with your left fingers, catch the yarn again with the hook.

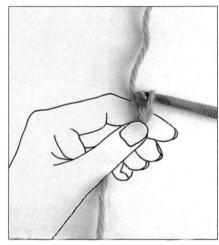

4 Draw the yarn on the hook back through the previous chain to make a new chain.

5 Repeat the last two steps to make the desired number of chains.

How to Begin
Double Chain

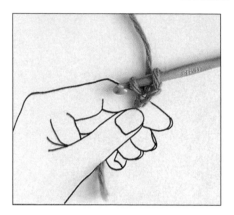

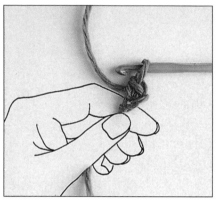

1 After you have completed 3 chains (as on previous page), insert the hook into the first chain you made and draw up a loop; there are 2 loops on the hook.

2 Catch the yarn with the hook and draw it through both loops on the hook; 1 loop remains on the hook.

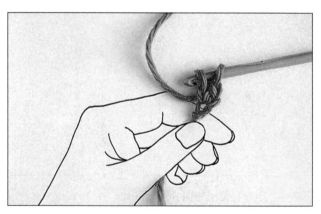

3 Insert the hook into the left edge strand of the double chain just made and draw up a loop; 2 loops remain on hook.

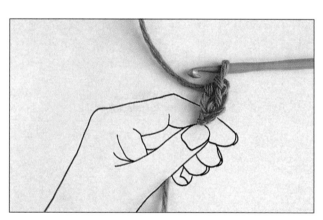

4 Catch the yarn with the hook and draw it through both loops; 1 loop remains on the hook.

5 Continue to repeat the last two steps for the desired number of double chains.

Basic Stitches 1
Single Crochet (sc)

1 When you have completed the desired number of stitches of your foundation chain, you are ready to work the first row of single crochet. Skip the last chain made and insert the hook into the next chain; hook the yarn and draw up a loop.

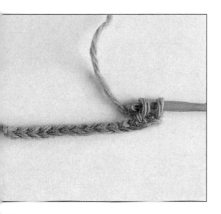

2 There are 2 loops on the hook. Catch the yarn over the hook again.

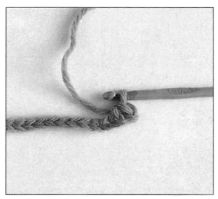

3 Draw the yarn through both loops on the hook. A single crochet is completed and 1 loop remains on the hook.

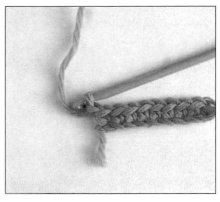

4 Repeat these steps to draw up a loop and make a single crochet (sc) in each remaining chain of the foundation chain. Make 1 chain stitch and turn work.

5 Work a single crochet in each single crochet of previous row, inserting hook under the 2 top threads of each sc to draw up yarn loop for new stitch. At end of row, chain 1; turn.

6 To fasten off on last row on work, cut yarn and draw yarn end through last loop. Tighten to keep yarn from unraveling. Sample shows single crochet stitch.

Basic Stitches 1
Single Crochet Rib Stitch

First Variation

1 This variation of the basic single crochet stitch forms a ribbed pattern. After the first row, work the single crochet stitches by inserting the hook under *only the front* strand at the top of each sc (of previous row) to draw up yarn loop for new stitch.

2 Complete each sc as you go in the usual way with a yarn over hook and draw through both loops on hook. The result is a softer crochet piece with slightly taller rows. Horizontal lines will show on each side.

Second Variation

1 You can also form a ribbed pattern by working single crochet stitches, after the first row, by inserting the hook under *only the back* top strand of each sc (of the previous row) to draw up a loop.

2 Yarn over (yo) and complete each stitch as before. This pattern tends to ripple more than the previous variation, giving a more pronounced ribbing.

Third Variation

1 Another variation alternates the two previous methods, working a row in the front strand, then the next row in the back strand of the sc row below. This method also produces a softer piece.

2 This sample of the third method shows the reverse side.

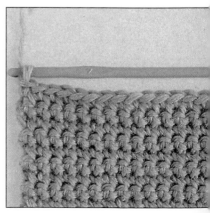

12

Basic Stitches 2
Slip Stitch (sl st)

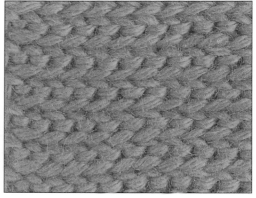

1 Insert the hook under both strands of the stitch below, yarn over hook to draw up a loop, and, in one continuous motion, draw it on through the loop on the hook.

2 This is a sample of slip stitch. The stitches are tightly packed and firm.

Variation (worked in rib)

1 Work slip stitches by inserting the hook under only the back loop of the stitch on the previous row to draw up loop and bring it on through the loop on the hook.

2 Continuing working in this manner for as many rows as desired.

3 This is a sample of this variation: a fabric stitch which resembles knitted stockinette stitch.

Slip stitch can also be used to reinforce a piece or provide a firm edge (with some slight elasticity) so that it will not stretch out of shape.

This sample shows a crocheted piece with a contrasting slip stitch border.

Basic Stitches 2
Half Double Crochet (hdc)

1 Work on a foundation chain or row of single crochet. Chain 2 and turn work. Wrap yarn over hook, then insert hook (under both top strands) in next stitch; hook yarn and draw up a loop (3 loops on hook).

2 Yarn over hook again and draw through all 3 loops on hook in one continuous motion to complete the half double crochet. Continue across row in this manner.

3 This is a sample piece worked in rows of half double crochet. This stitch is less dense than single crochet.

First Variation (worked in front strand)

Work half double crochet stitch by inserting the hook into the front strand (loop) only of the stitch below. You will make horizontal ridges across rows as shown.

Second Variation (worked in back strand)

Work half double crochet stitch by inserting the hook into the back strand (loop) only of the stitch below. The piece should look like the sample above.

Basic Stitches 3
Double Crochet (dc)

1 Work on a foundation chain or a row of single crochet. Chain 3, turn work. Wrap yarn over hook and insert hook (under both top strands) in next stitch; hook yarn and draw up a loop (3 loops on hook).

2 Yarn over hook and draw through first 2 loops on hook (2 loops remain on hook).

3 Yarn over again and draw through the 2 remaining loops on hook to complete the double crochet stitch (1 loop remains on hook). Continue across row in this manner.

As before, you can vary the look of the stitch by inserting the hook under only the front or only the back loop of the stitch below rather than under both loops (strands). The sample above shows the double crochet stitches worked under both loops, as it is most commonly worked.

Another variation is to insert the hook into the space *between* 2 double crochet stitches of the previous row to work a new row of double crochet. It produces a more open look and appears the same on both sides.

Basic Stitches 3
Treble (tr)

1 Work on a foundation chain or row. Chain 4, turn work. Yarn over twice, insert hook into next stitch, yarn over, and draw up a loop (4 loops on hook).

2 Yarn over and draw through first 2 loops on hook (3 loops remain on hook).

3 Yarn over and draw through next 2 loops on hook (2 loops remain on hook).

4 Yarn over and draw through next 2 loops on hook to complete treble (1 loop remains on hook).

5 The sample is worked in treble. Work double treble (dtr) with yarn over three times and treble treble (tr tr) with yarn over four times; work off loops two by two.

How to Turn Work

In order to crochet back and forth in rows, it is necessary to add extra chains (called turning chains) before turning the work. This allows the hook to rise to the proper height to begin the next row and keeps the edges from pulling in.

The turning chain for the taller stitches forms the first stitch of the next row. The number of chains to work varies with the stitch being used.

Single Crochet = 1 chain
Half Double Crochet = 2 chains
Double Crochet = 3 chains
Treble = 4 chains
Double Treble = 5 chains
Treble Treble = 6 chains

Starting in Rounds
How to Work the Center Ring (First Method)

Many projects, such as berets, doilies, and floral motifs, are worked around in circular rows, beginning with a center ring. You will increase the number of stitches on each row to keep the work flat or shaped as the project directions indicate.

1 Begin with the desired number of chains. To join them to form a ring, insert the hook into the first chain worked.

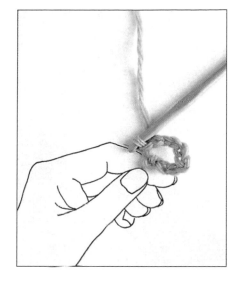

2 Yarn over and draw it through the loop on the hook (this is called joining with a slip stitch). You have formed the foundation chain for the center ring.

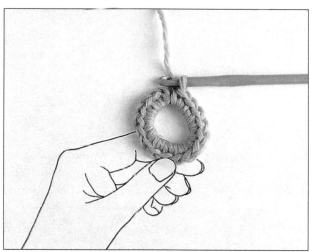

3 Chain 1, then work a single crochet (sc) by inserting the hook into the center hole of the ring to draw up a loop; complete sc as before (sc encloses the chain ring). Continue to work sc in this manner around the ring until you have the desired number of sc (usually about one and one half times the number of chains made for the center ring).

4 Join the last sc worked to the beginning chain (or to first single crochet if directions so indicate) with a slip stitch to complete the round (rnd).

5 This is how the center ring should look with 1 round of single crochet completed.

Starting in Rounds
How to Work the Center Ring (Second Method)

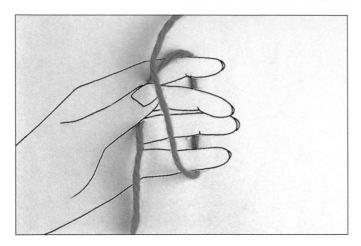

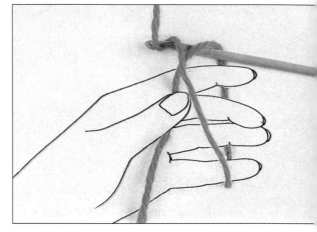

1 Holding the yarn end with your thumb and index finger, wrap the ball of yarn down around the back of your hand and up the palm as shown.

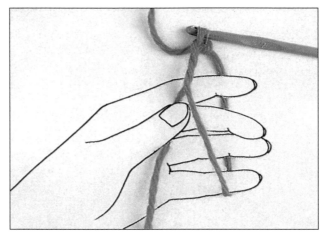

2 Insert the hook through the yarn loop from the front and yarn over.

3 Draw the loop forward to form the ring and work 1 chain stitch.

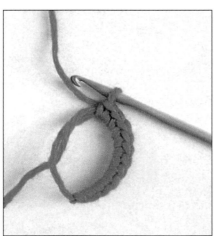

4 Work a single crochet (sc) by inserting hook into center of ring to draw up a loop; complete sc as before. Continue to work sc in this manner around ring, enclosing ring within sc stitches.

5 Complete the desired number of sc and tighten the ring by pulling the yarn end. Join to the beginning sc with a slip stitch to complete center ring.

Working in Rounds
Working Around on a Foundation Ring of 6 Chains

A Round in Half Double Crochet (1 rnd of hdc)

Follow steps 1 and 2 of the first method (page 17) to make a foundation ring of 6 chains. Chain 2 (ch 2), then yarn over hook and insert hook into ring to work a half double crochet (hdc). Work 11 more hdc in ring. Join with slip stitch (sl st) to top chain of ch-2 at beginning to complete rnd. Note that 2 hdc are worked for each ch of the ring. For sc, the beginning chain does not count as a stitch, but for hdc, as here, it may.

A Round in Double Crochet (1 rnd of dc)

Make a foundation ring as before. Chain 3 (ch 3), then work 14 double crochet (dc) by inserting hook into ring. Join with a slip stitch (sl st) to top chain of ch-3 at beginning to complete rnd. Counting the ch-3 as the first stitch, note that there are 2.5 dc for each ch of the foundation chain; for dc and all taller stitches, the beginning ch counts as a stitch.

A Round in Treble (1 rnd of tr)

Make a foundation ring as before. Chain 4 (ch 4), then work 19 treble (tr) in ring. Join with a slip stitch (sl st) to top of ch-4 to complete rnd.

Counting the ch-4 as the first stitch, note that there are 3 tr for each ch of the foundation ring, plus 2 more.

A Round in Double Crochet Alternating with Chain [1 rnd of (dc, ch 1)]

Make a foundation ring as before. Chain 4 (this counts as first dc and ch 1), then work 1 double crochet and 1 chain (dc, ch 1) 9 times. Join with a slip stitch (sl st) to the third chain of the ch-4 to complete rnd. Counting the ch-4 as the first pair, note that there are 10 pairs of dc and ch-1.

A Round in Treble Alternating with Chain [1 rnd of (tr, ch 1)]

Make foundation ring as before. Chain 5 (counts as first tr and ch 1), then work 1 treble and 1 chain (tr, ch 1) 11 times. Join with a slip stitch (sl st) to the fourth chain of the ch-5 to complete rnd.

Counting the ch-5 as the first pair, note that there are 12 pairs of tr and ch-1.

Working in Squares
How to Work the First Row

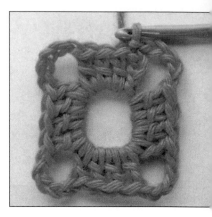

A Square in Double Crochet (dc)

Follow steps 1 and 2 of the first method (page 17) to make a foundation ring of 6 chains. Chain 3 (ch 3, counts as first stitch) by inserting hook into center of ring, work 2 double crochet (dc), chain 3 for corner, * work 3 dc, ch 3 *; repeat instructions from first * to second * twice more. Join with a slip stitch (sl st) to the top of the beginning ch-3 to complete row.

Variation of Square in Double Crochet (dc)

Make a foundation ring as before. Chain 3 (ch-3 counts as first stitch), work 3 double crochet (dc) in ring, chain 2 for corner, * work 4 dc in ring, ch 2 *; repeat from * to * twice more. Join with sl st to top of ch-3 to complete row.

A Filet Square in Double Crochet (dc)

Make a foundation ring of 12 chains. Chain 3 (first stitch), work 3 double crochet (dc) in ring, chain 5 for corner, * work 4 dc in ring, ch 5 *; repeat from * to * twice more. Join with sl st to top of ch-3 to complete row.

Variation of Square in Double Crochet (dc)

1 Make a foundation ring of 13 chains. Then chain 5 more, work a dc into fourth chain (ch) of foundation ring, ch 3, rotate work, then inserting hook under dc just made, work 2 dc over it (original dc is enclosed in base of these 2 new dc).

2 * Make a dc in same ch of foundation ring as the enclosed dc to complete the block of stitches. Then ch 2, skip next 2 ch of foundation ring, dc in next ch of foundation ring, ch 3, rotate work, insert hook under dc just made to work 2 dc (enclosing dc in new stitches)*. Repeat from * to * twice more. Join with a sl st to third ch of beginning ch-5 to complete row.

Increasing
Single Increases (inc)

1 To add a stitch within the work, simply work 1 stitch as usual and then make another stitch in the same place (2 stitches worked in one stitch of the previous row).

2 Mark the position of the addition with a contrasting colored yarn, as shown, or a safety pin to facilitate the placement of other increases.

3 For increasing on each row, work the increase on the first stitch of the previous row's addition. Continue in this manner so the increases appear in a regular pattern. The piece will form a point after several rows of increasing at the same place.

Single Increase at Beginning of Row

Work turning chain (see page 16) as usual, then for sc and hdc, work 2 stitches in first stitch of previous row. Note that for dc and all taller stitches, turning chain counts as first stitch, so for them work only 1 additional stitch in first stitch of previous row. The edge of piece will slant outward.

Single Increases at Beginning and End of Row

Work increase at beginning of work as before, then work across row to last stitch, work 2 stitches in last stitch. Both edges will slant outward. The more frequent the increases at an edge, the more pronounced the degree of the slant.

Increasing
Multiple increases

Multiple Increases at Beginning of Row

1 To add several stitches to a row (as for a sleeve), chain a number of stitches equal to the number of stitches to be added at the end of the last row *before* increase row.

2 Add chains for turning chain (2, in this case, for half double crochet). Leaving turning chain stitches unworked, work a stitch (hdc shown) in each remaining chain stitch that was added. Complete row in pattern.

Multiple Increases at End of Row

1 An easy method (not shown) is to attach a separate strand of matching yarn and chain the desired number of stitches, then with main yarn continue working pattern across these added chains.

For a more professional method, work as follows: work to end of established row (hdc shown), then yarn over; insert hook under lower left strand of last stitch just completed and work another stitch (hdc, in this case).

2 Repeat this step, working a new stitch through the lower left strand of the previous stitch, until you have the desired number of added stitches.

3 This increase makes a softer edge than the one described above for the beginning of a row. By turning work around, you can increase this way at either the end or the beginning of a row.

Decreasing
Single Decreases (First Method)

Decreasing is used to lessen the width of a piece. You can decrease at the edges or within the work. Decreases can be single or multiple. They are often worked at the edges of the piece, as at underarm seams or around neck edges. Used within a piece, decreases can provide special shaping, as darts do on sewn garments.

1 To decrease at the beginning of a row, work as follows: Add chains for turning chain (2, in this case, for half double crochet), skip a stitch for first decrease, work stitch (hdc shown) in next stitch, and work across row to last 2 stitches.

2 To decrease at the end of a row, skip the next-to-last stitch, work a stitch in the last stitch.

3 To decrease in the middle of a row, skip a stitch and work the next one. Mark the beginning point of a decrease with yarn (as shown) or a safety pin to align other decreases accurately.

4 If the decreases are worked only at the beginning of rows, the piece will slant inward.

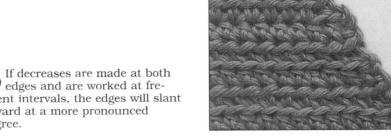

5 If decreases are made at both edges and are worked at frequent intervals, the edges will slant inward at a more pronounced degree.

Decreasing
Decreasing Several Stitches Together

1 To decrease several stitches at the beginning of the row, work a slip stitch in each stitch to be decreased.

2 Slip stitch in next stitch and chain 3 (for double crochet, in this case, or as needed for other stitches) for first stitch, then work across row to end.

3 To make decreases at end of row, simply leave desired number of stitches unworked at end of row.

4 Make turning chain and turn work around to crochet next row back across remaining stitches.

5 If decreases are to be made within a row (as for a neckline), work across row to start of decrease section. Make a turning chain (or work as directed), turn work to complete one side of piece. Then skip the center stitches to be decreased, attach yarn to the next stitch, work as directed to complete second side to correspond to the first.

Decreasing
Single Decreases (Second Method)

Decreases can be done by working 2 stitches together at the edges or within the piece. This makes a more compact work without the small openings that can show when a stitch is skipped.

Single Crochet (sc)

1 To work a decrease in single crochet, draw up a loop in the next stitch, then draw up another loop in the following stitch (3 loops on hook).

2 Yarn over and, in one motion, draw the loop through all 3 loops on the hook (1 sc is worked over 2 stitches for the decrease). Mark position of decreases made within work.

2 Yarn over and, in one motion, draw the loop through all 5 loops on the hook. Mark position of decreases made within work.

Half Double Crochet (hdc)

1 To work a decrease in half double crochet, yarn over, then insert hook in next stitch and draw up a loop (3 loops on hook); yarn over and draw up a loop in the following stitch (5 loops on hook).

Double Crochet (dc)

1 To work a decrease in double crochet, yarn over and draw up a loop in the next stitch (3 loops on hook); yarn over and draw through first 2 loops on hook (2 loops on hook); yarn over and draw up a loop in the following stitch (4 loops on hook); yarn over and draw through first 2 loops on hook (3 loops on hook).

2 Yarn over and, in one motion, draw loop through all 3 loops on hook. Mark position of decreases made within work.

Decreasing
Single Decreases (Second Method)

Treble (tr)

1 To work a decrease in treble, yarn over twice, then draw up a loop in the next stitch (4 loops on hook); yarn over and draw through first 2 loops on hook; yarn over and draw through next 2 loops on hook (2 loops on hook).

2 Yarn over twice and draw up a loop in the following stitch (5 loops on hook).

3 Yarn over and draw through first 2 loops on hook; yarn over and draw through next 2 loops on hook (3 loops on hook).

4 Yarn over and, in one motion, draw through all 3 loops on hook.

Afghan (Tunisian) Stitch

Afghan (also called Tunisian) stitch is worked on a long hook that holds the stitches as you work across a row. It differs from regular crocheting because you work a row in two stages: first you draw up a loop for each stitch across the row, then you work each stitch off the hook as you work back to the beginning end of the row.

1 Begin with desired number of chains, working rather loosely to make a foundation chain in the usual manner. Insert the hook into the second chain from the hook and draw up a loop. Leave the loop on the hook.

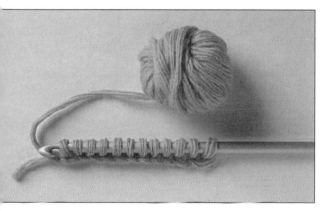

2 Continue to draw up a loop in each chain across, leaving each new loop on the hook. At the end of the first row, there should be as many loops as there are chains.

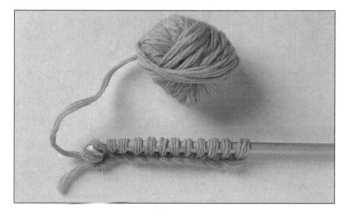

3 Yarn over and draw the loop through the first loop sitting on the hook. (Once worked, this loop will drop from the hook.)

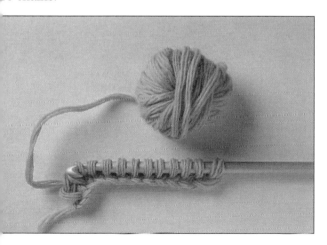

4 Yarn over and draw through 2 loops (the new loop just made and the next loop sitting on the hook).

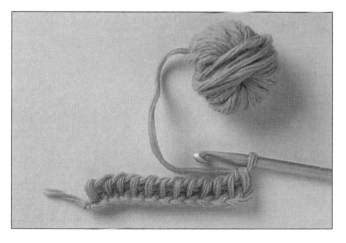

5 Repeat across this (return) row until only 1 loop remains on hook; this loop becomes the first vertical stitch on the next row.

Afghan (Tunisian) Stitch

6 To start the next row, skip this first stitch, then insert the hook right to left under the front vertical strand of the next stitch on the row below and draw up a loop to remain on the hook.

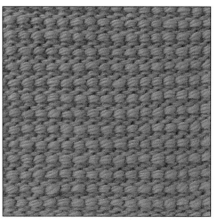

7 Continue in this manner to draw up a loop through the vertical strand of each stitch across row, retaining the loops on the hook.

8 Repeat steps 3 through 5 to complete the return row. Work in afghan stitch to desired length. On last row, slip stitch in each vertical strand across row. Fasten off.

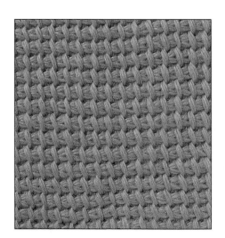

9 The sample above shows the front, or right side, of afghan stitch.

10 This sample shows the reverse, or wrong side.

Variations of the Afghan (Tunisian) Stitch

Afghan Stockinette Stitch

1 Make a foundation chain and work the first 2 rows as for afghan stitch (see pages 27–28). **Row 3**: Chain 1, * insert hook from front to back between the front and back vertical strands of the next stitch and draw up a loop *. Retaining loops on hook, repeat from * to * across row.

2 **Row 4**: Work this return row as for regular afghan stitch (see steps 3 through 5, page 27). Repeat these 2 rows for pattern. This afghan knit stitch looks much like a knitted stockinette stitch, but has a very firm texture.

3 The sample shows the reverse side of the work. Its firmness makes it well suited for cold and windy weather garments.

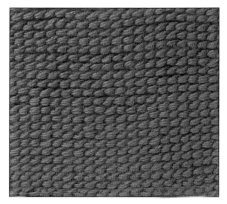

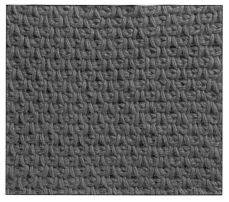

Afghan Tweed Stitch

1 Make a foundation chain with an uneven number of chains. Work the first 2 rows as for afghan stitch. **Row 3**: Skip first stitch as usual, * insert hook from right to left through the next vertical strand and draw up a loop, then insert hook from left to right through following vertical strand and draw up a loop without twisting the yarn *; repeat from * to * across. **Row 4**: Work this return row as usual.

2 **Row 5**: * Insert hook left to right in the next stitch and draw up loop without twisting yarn, then insert hook right to left in following stitch and draw up loop *; repeat from * to * across. **Row 6**: Work return row as usual. Repeat these last 4 rows for pattern. Sample above shows the pattern.

Variations of the Afghan (Tunisian) Stitch

Afghan Stitch on the Bias

1 Make foundation chain with an uneven number of stitches. Work first 2 rows as for afghan stitch. **Row 3**: Skip first stitch as usual, * then skip next stitch, insert hook through vertical strand of next stitch and draw up loop; then draw up loop in skipped stitch in same manner *; repeat from * to * across. **Row 4**: Work return row as usual.

2 **Row 5**: Working through vertical strands, draw up loop in next stitch, * skip next stitch, draw up loop in following stitch, then draw up loop in skipped stitch *; repeat across row to last stitch, draw up loop in last stitch. **Row 6**: Work return row as usual. Repeat last 4 rows. The right side of work shows diagonal line.

Afghan Lace

1 Make a foundation chain with a number of chains that is a multiple of 4, plus 1. **Row 1**: Draw up a loop in second and each remaining chain as usual. **Row 2 (return row)**: Chain 3 in last loop on hook, then yarn over and draw through first 5 loops on hook, * chain 4, yarn over, and draw through the next 5 loops on hook *; repeat from * to * across row, ending with a chain.

2 **Row 3**: * Draw up a loop in each chain (working in 1 chain on top of cluster of stitches and in each of 3 chains between clusters) *; repeat across row. You should have the same number as starting chain.

3 Repeat Rows 2 and 3 for pattern stitch. The sample shows how the lace pattern looks when it is completed.

Net Stitch

The crocheted net stitch is the basis of several other pattern stitches. It becomes filet crochet when solid blocks of stitches are combined with the open spaces of the net stitch to form decorative patterns. It can form the background for Irish lace motifs and other lace patterns.

Open Net Stitch

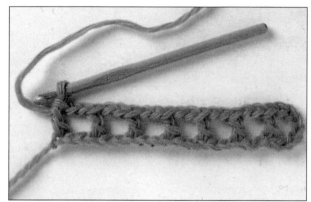

1 Make a foundation chain (ch) with a multiple of 3. **Row 1**: Ch 5, work a double crochet (dc) in eighth ch from hook, * ch 2, skip next 2 ch of foundation ch, dc in next ch *; repeat from * to * across. Ch 5, turn work. (This turning ch-5 will count as first dc and ch-2 on next row.)

2 **Row 2**: Skip first dc, dc in next dc, * ch 2, dc in next dc *; repeat from * to * across, ending with dc in 3rd ch. Ch 5; turn work.

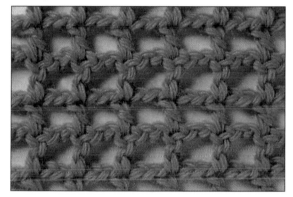

3 Continue to repeat Row 2 for pattern stitch. This sample shows how the net stitch looks.

Alternating Block Net Stitch

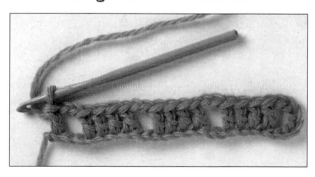

1 Make a foundation chain with a multiple of 6, plus 3. **Row 1**: Ch 5, dc in 8th ch from hook, dc in each of next 3 ch (first block made), * ch 2, skip next 2 ch of foundation ch, work dc in each of next 4 ch (another block made) *; repeat from * to * across last 3 ch, then ch 2, skip 2 ch, dc in last ch. Ch 3, turn. (Turning ch is first stitch on next row.)

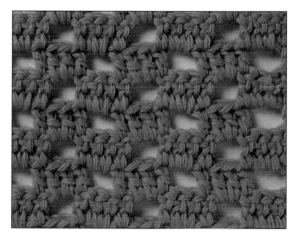

2 Continue in rows, alternating blocks of 4 dc (dc in dc, 2 dc over ch-2, dc in dc) with open spaces formed by ch-2 as shown above.

Increasing in Net Stitch

At the Beginning of an Open Net Row

At end of row, work ch-5 and turn as usual. Increase row: Work dc in first dc of last row (1 open space added), complete row. To increase by several squares, make 3 extra ch at end of row for each extra open space to be added. For example, to add 3 spaces, ch 5 (initial space), ch 6 more (spaces 2 and 3). Then dc in sixth ch from hook, ch 2, skip 2 ch, dc in next ch, ch 2, skip 2 ch, dc in first dc of last row.

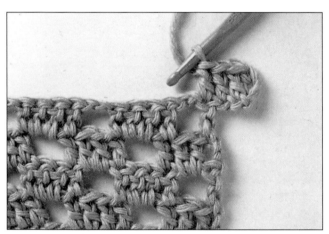

At the Beginning of Alternating Block Row

At end of row, chain 5 and turn work. Increase row: Dc in fourth ch from hook, dc in next ch, dc in first dc of last row (1 block added), complete row. To increase by several blocks, make 6 extra ch at end of row for each extra pair (block plus open space) added to first added block.

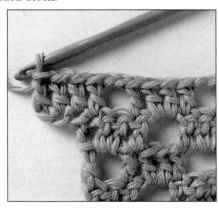

At End of Open Net Row

At end of row, work ch 2, then work double treble (dtr) in same place where last dc was worked. Ch 5, turn work, and work as usual. To increase by several open spaces, repeat (ch 2 and work dtr at center bend of last dtr made) until you have desired number.

At End of Alternating Block Row

1 At end of row, * yarn over, insert hook under strand at base of last dc and draw up loop; yarn over and draw through first loop on hook, then complete dc as usual *.

2 Repeat from * to * twice more to complete block. Work turning chain and continue as normal for next row.

Variations of Net Stitch

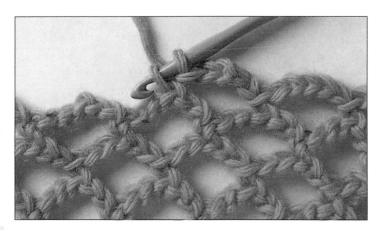

Diamond Net Stitch

1 Make a foundation chain with a number of chains that is a multiple of 4, plus 2. **Row 1**: Sc in second ch from hook, * ch 5, skip 3 ch of foundation, sc in next ch *; repeat from * to * across foundation chain. Ch 7, turn. **Row 2**: * Sc in third ch (at center of) first ch-5 arch, ch 5 *; repeat from * to * across, ending with sc in third ch of last arch, then ch 2, work dtr in last stitch. Ch 6, turn. **Row 3**: Sc in third ch of first ch-5 arch, * ch 5, sc in third ch of next arch *; repeat from * to * across. Ch 7, turn. Repeat Rows 2 and 3 for pattern.

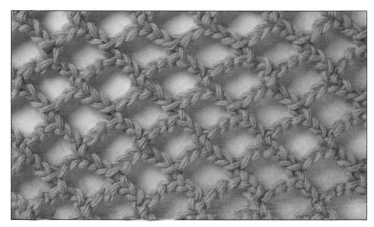

2 The photograph shows a sample of diamond net stitch. This stitch works well for flat pieces as well as for pieces worked in rounds because it is loose and flexible. It can also be used for joining fabric to lace borders.

Hexagonal Net Stitch

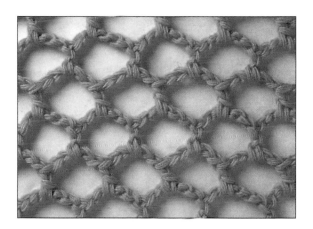

1 Make chain that is a multiple of 5. **Row 1**: Ch 8 (counts as first dc and ch-5 arch, dc in 13th ch from hook, * ch 5, skip 4 ch, dc in next ch *; repeat from * to * across. Ch 6, turn. **Row 2**: * Yarn over, insert hook into space below next arch and work dc (enclosing arch in base of dc), ch 5 *; repeat from * to * across, ending with dc over last arch, ch 3, tr in 3rd ch of turning chain. Ch 8, turn.

2 **Row 3**: Skip first ch-3 arch, * dc over next ch-5 arch, ch 5 *; repeat from * to * across, ending with dc in the fifth ch of turning ch. Ch 6, turn. Repeat Rows 2 and 3 for pattern.

Photograph shows a sample of hexagonal net stitch. It is often used as a background for Irish lace.

Variations of Net Stitch

Lily Net Stitch

1 Make a foundation chain that is a multiple of 12. **Row 1**: Ch 5, sc in eighth ch from hook, ch 2, skip 2 foundation ch, dc in next ch, * ch 5, skip 5 ch, dc in next ch, ch 2, skip 2 ch, sc in next ch, ch 2, skip 2 ch, dc in next ch *; repeat from * to * across, ending with ch 5, skip 5 ch, dc in last ch. Ch 5, turn. **Row 2**: Sc over first ch-5 arch, *ch 2, dc in next dc, ch 5, dc in next dc, ch 2, sc over next arch *; repeat from * to *, ending ch 2, dc in next dc, ch 5, dc in third ch of turning ch. Repeat Row 2 for pattern.

Bridge Net Stitch

1 Make foundation ch with multiple of 6. **Row 1**: Ch 5, sc in eighth ch from hook, ch 2, skip 2 foundation ch, dc in next ch, * ch 2, skip 2 ch, sc in next ch, ch 2, skip 2 ch, dc in next ch *; repeat from * to * across. Ch 8, turn. **Row 2**: Skip first dc at base of ch-8, * dc in next dc, ch 5 *; repeat from * to * across, ending skip top 2 ch of turning ch, dc in next ch of turning ch. Ch 5, turn. **Row 3**: Sc over first ch-5 arch, * ch 2, dc in next dc, ch 2, sc over next arch *; repeat from * to * across, ending ch 2, dc in third ch of ch-8. Ch 8, turn. Repeat Rows 2 and 3 for pattern.

2 This is a sample of completed lily net stitch.

2 Photograph shows sample of bridge n stitch.

34

Geometric Shapes

Geometric shapes are the basis for many projects—from hats, jackets, and whimsical vests to afghans, pillows, placemats, and other practical household items. Increases (see page 21) are used to shape the pieces.

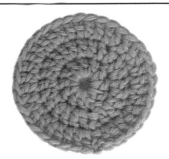

Circle

Chain 6 and join with sl st to form a ring (see page 17). Work in rounds as follows:

Rnd 1: Ch 2 (counts as first hdc), work 11 hdc in ring; join with sl st to top of ch-2 (12 hdc).

Rnd 2: Ch 2, work hdc in first hdc below, work 2 hdc in each remaining hdc; join as before (24 hdc).

Rnd 3: Ch 2, work 2 hdc in next hdc (inc made), * hdc in next hdc, 2 hdc in next hdc *; repeat from * to * around (12 inc made). Continue to work around making inc evenly spaced on each rnd. Make 6 to 12 inc as needed to keep work flat. To keep edge of work rounded (not pointed), alternate position of inc and avoid working inc directly above inc of previous rnd.

Variation of Circle

For this circle, do not join as before, but continue to work around in a spiral. Mark first stitch of rnd with a safety pin and move pin with each new rnd. Ch 5 and join to form ring.

Rnd 1: Work 9 sc in ring.

Rnd 2: Continuing right around, work 2 sc in each sc (18 sc).

Rnd 3: Work * sc in next sc, 2 sc in next sc (inc made) *; repeat from * to * around (9 inc made). Continue to work around, making 6 to 9 inc evenly spaced around, keeping work flat (rippled work indicates too many inc), and alternating position of inc.

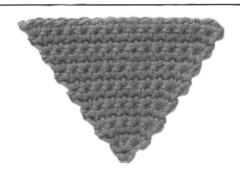

Triangle

Start at lower point and work back and forth in rows. Ch 2, turn work.

Row 1: Sc in second ch from hook. Ch 1, turn.

Row 2: Work 3 sc in sc. Ch 1, turn.

Row 3: Work 2 sc in first sc (inc made), sc in next sc, 2 sc in last sc (another inc). Ch 1, turn.

Row 4: Sc in each sc. Ch 1, turn.

Row 5: Inc in first sc as before, sc in each sc to last sc, inc in last sc as before (2 inc made on row). Ch 1, turn.

Repeat Rows 4 and 5 until triangle is desired size.

Square

Work back and forth in rows. Ch 2.

Row 1: Work 3 sc in second ch from hook. Ch 1, turn.

Row 2: Sc in first sc, 3 sc in next sc (2-sc inc made), sc in last sc (5 sc in all). Ch 1, turn.

Row 3: Sc in each of first 2 sc, 3 sc in next sc (at center), sc in each of last 2 sc. Ch 1, turn.

Row 4: Sc in each sc to center sc, work 3 sc in center sc, sc in each sc to end. Ch 1, turn.

Repeat Row 4 until square is desired size.

Geometric Shapes

Square Worked in Rounds
Ch 3 and join with sl st to form a ring.
Rnd 1: Ch 1 (beginning ch does not count as a stitch), work (sc, then ch 1) four times in ring. Join with sl st to first sc.
Rnd 2: Ch 1, * sc in sc, work (sc, ch 1 and sc) over next ch-1 (corner made) *, repeat from * to * three more times. Join with sl st to first sc.
Rnd 3: Continue in this manner to work sc in each sc and work (sc, ch 1, sc) over each corner ch-1. Join last sc with sl st to first sl st. (Joining will fall at center of one side of square.)
Repeat Row 3 until square is desired size.

Variation of Square Worked in Rounds
Ch 6 and join with sl st to form ring.
Rnd 1: Ch 3 (counts as first dc), work 2 dc in ring, ch 2, * work 3 dc in ring, ch 2 *; repeat from * to * twice more. Join with sl st to top of ch-3.
Rnd 2: Ch 3, dc in next 2 dc, work (dc, ch 2, dc) over next ch-2 (corner made), * dc in next 3 dc, work corner as before *; repeat from * to * twice more. Join as before.
Rnd 3: Work dc in each dc and work (dc, ch 2, dc) over each corner ch-2. Join.
Repeat Row 3 until square is desired size.

Pentagon
Ch 4 and join with sl st to form ring.
Rnd 1: Ch 2 (counts as first hdc), hdc in ring, ch 2, * 2 hdc in ring, ch 2 *; repeat from * to * three more times. Join with sl st to top of first ch-2.
Rnd 2: Ch 2, hdc in hdc, work (hdc, ch 2, hdc) over next ch-2 (corner made), * hdc in 2 hdc, work corner as before *; repeat from * to * three more times. Join as before.
Rnd 3: Work hdc in each hdc and work (hdc, ch 2, hdc) over each corner ch-2. Join. Repeat Row 3 until pentagon is desired size.

Hexagon
Ch 4 and join with sl st to form ring.
Rnd 1: Ch 1 (does not count as sc), work 12 sc in ring. Join with sl st to first sc.
Rnd 2: Ch 2 (counts as first hdc), work (hdc, ch 2, hdc) in next sc (for corner), * hdc in next sc, work (hdc, ch 2, hdc) on next sc (corner) *; repeat from * to * four more times. Join to top of ch-2.
Rnd 3: Work hdc in each hdc and work (hdc, ch 2, hdc) over each corner ch-2. Join. Repeat Rnd 3 until hexagon is desired size.

Edgings

Edgings or borders complete a work of crochet by refining the work and adding decoration. They can even be added to knitted or fabric pieces. The edgings can be worked directly on a piece, or worked separately and attached when completed. Often the same yarn is used for the trim, but contrasting colors can also be used.

1 When an edging is added directly to the piece, it is best to work a row of single crochet around the piece to stabilize the edges. Sc in each stitch of the top and bottom rows and sc along the side edges, making a stitch in row (as in this case, with sc rows), or as needed to keep side edges flat without pulling in or stretching.

Reverse Single Crochet Edging

1 Work a row of sc at edge of piece with right side of work facing you. Join if a rnd, but do not turn work. **Reverse single crochet row:** * Working from left to right, work as follows: draw up loop in next sc to the right (2 loops on hook).

2 Yarn over (yo) and draw loop through both loops on hook (reverse sc made) *; repeat from * to * all around edge. Join. Photograph shows completed border. This edging gives a firm but very attractive finish.

Picot Edging

1 At edge, work a row of sc with a multiple of 3, plus 1. Join and continue to work in rounds, if possible; or cut yarn and fasten off at end of first row and reattach yarn to start of first row without turning work.
Picot Row: Ch 1, sc in first 2 sc, * ch 4, sl st in first ch of ch-4 (picot made).

2 Then sc in next 3 sc *; repeat from * to * along first row, ending with sc in last 2 sc.

Edgings

Cluster Edging

1 Work a row of sc at edge of piece. **Cluster Row**: Starting at beginning of row just completed, sc in first sc, * hdc in next sc, then (yarn over and insert hook between hdc just made and previous stitch to draw up a loop) twice (5 loops on hook).

2 Insert hook into back loop only at top of next sc, yarn over (yo), and draw through all loops on hook in one motion (completed cluster lies sideways, enclosing hdc) *; repeat from * to * along row of sc. This border is compact, yet soft, and is well suited for classic and elegant pieces.

Twisted Edging

1 At edge, work a row of sc with a multiple of 3, plus 1. **Row 2**: Starting at beginning of row just completed, ch 1, sc in first sc, * ch 3, skip 2 sc, sc in next sc *; repeat from * to * along first row of sc. Cut yarn and fasten off. **Contrasting Row**: Using a contrasting colored yarn and starting again at the beginning of the last row, ch 2 and sc in first sc of previous row, ch 3, *remove hook from last ch and insert the hook under the next ch-3 of the previous row; pick up the dropped chain of contrasting color (being careful not to undo any chains).

2 Ch 4 *; repeat from * to * along previous row, ending with ch 3 and sc in last sc. This edging works well for baby items.

Scalloped Edging

1 With contrasting colored yarn, work row of sc. **Row 2**: Starting again at beginning of row just completed, ch and sc in first sc, * ch 3, then in same place where sc was just worked, (yarn over and draw up a loop; yarn over and draw through first two loops on hook) twice (3 loops on hook).

2 Yarn over and draw through all 3 loops on hook, skip next 3 sc, sc in next sc *; repeat from * to * along previous row. This is a soft and feminine edging.

Lace Border Made to Desired Length

Borders can be worked sideways (back and forth in rows) for the desired length. The foundation chain determines the width of the finished lace; the number of rows worked determines the length of the lace border. Borders made this way are worked as a separate piece that is attached to the main piece upon completion.

Festoons

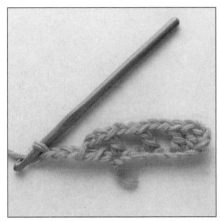

1 Ch 11 for foundation. Dc in fourth ch from hook, dc in next ch, ch 2, skip 2 ch, dc in next ch, ch 2, skip 2 ch, work (dc, ch 3 and dc) in last ch. Ch 5, turn.

2 Work (3 dc, ch 1, 3 dc) over ch-3 arch (called ch-3 loop in some directions), ch 2, skip dc at base of arch, dc in next dc, ch 2, dc in next 2 dc, dc in top of ch-3. Ch 3, turn.

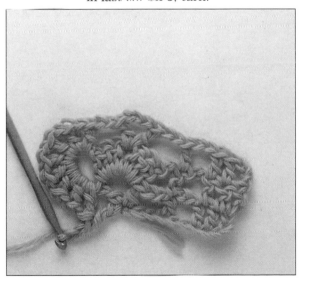

3 Skip first dc, dc in next 2 dc, ch 2, dc in next dc, ch 2, work (dc, ch 3, dc) over in ch-1 arch between 3-dc groups, ch 2, work (dc, ch 1) seven times over turning ch-5, dc over same ch-5, tr in first ch of foundation ch (at end of first row). Ch 2, turn.

4 Sc over ch-1 arch between first 2 dc below, work (ch 3, sc over next ch-1 between 2 dc) six more times, ch 2, work (3 dc, ch 1, 3 dc) over ch-3 arch between 2 dc, ch 2, skip dc at base of arch just worked, dc in next dc, ch 2, dc in last 3 dc (counting ch-3 as dc). Ch 3, turn.

Lace Border Made to Desired Length

5 Skip first dc, dc in next 2 dc, ch 2, dc in next dc, ch 2, work (dc, ch 3, dc) over ch-1 arch between 3-dc groups. Ch 5, turn.

6 Work (3 dc, ch 1, 3 dc) over ch-3 arch, ch 2, skip dc at arch, dc in next dc, ch 2, dc in last 3 dc. Ch 3, turn.

7 Skip first dc, dc in next 2 dc, ch 2, dc in next dc, ch 2, work (dc, ch 3, dc) over ch-1 arch between 3-dc groups, ch 2, work (dc, ch 1) seven times over ch-5, dc over same ch-5, sc over ch-2 after the 3-dc group (this ch-2 connects to previous festoon). Ch 2, turn.

8 Repeat steps 4 through 7 for pattern until lace border is the desired length. Cut yarn and fasten off. This border can by sewn by hand to edge of project using a backstitch. Sample shows complete festoon border.

Borders Worked in Rows

These ribbed borders are often used to begin crocheted sweaters. They are elastic enough to use for waistbands and wristbands.

Border Worked in Post Double Crochet

1 Make a foundation chain with an even number of stitches. Work 1 row of dc across foundation ch (see page 15). Ch 3, turn. **Row 2:** Skip first dc (ch-3 counts as first dc), then yarn over (yo) and insert hook front to back before next dc and bring hook tip out just after this same dc (dc lies across hook).

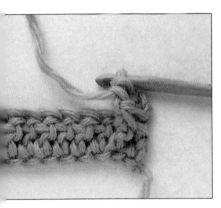

2 Yo, draw up loop, and complete dc as usual (base of dc is wrapped around post of dc below and front post dc is made).

3 Yo, reach behind work to insert hook back to front around post of next dc, bringing hook tip back out behind work.

4 Yo, draw loop through to back of work and complete dc (back post dc made).

5 Continue to work across row, alternating front and back post dc stitches, ending row with a dc in last dc. Ch 3, turn. Repeat Row 2 for pattern, always working the vertical stitches so they are raised on the same side of work to make the rib pattern as shown.

Borders Worked in Rows

Border Worked in Post Single Crochet

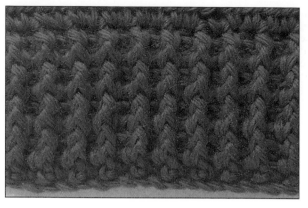

1 Chain an uneven number of ch. Work 1 row of sc (even number of sc made). Ch 1, turn. **Row 2**: Sc in first sc, insert hook from front around post of next sc, draw up loop, and complete sc (front post sc).

2 Inserting hook from back around next sc, work back post sc to correspond. Complete row, alternating front and back post sc, ending sc in last sc. Ch 1, turn. Repeat Row 2, for pattern, always working vertical stitches so they are raised to form rib pattern.

Easy Ribbing in Single Crochet

This ribbing is worked sideways. Chain number of stitches that will give desired height of ribbing border. Work in single crochet rib stitch, second variation (page 12), working rows back and forth until piece is desired length. To use as a waist-band, turn ribbing sideways to work a row of sc on one long edge (with correct multiple for pattern), then work sweater in desired pattern across this sc row.

Mock Ribbing with Post Stitches

1 Chain uneven number of stitches. **Row 1**: Hdc across. Ch 2 (do not count as hdc), turn. **Row 2**: Hdc in first hdc, * yo twice, then insert hook from front to back behind next hdc in row below; draw up a loop, yo, and complete tr (front post tr made).

2 Skip hdc where tr was made, hdc in next hdc *; repeat from * to * across. Ch 2, turn. Repeat these 2 rows for pattern until ribbing is desired height.

Hairpin Lace

This type of crocheting requires a special tool in addition to a crochet hook. The tool is called a hairpin because of its U shape. The hairpins come in different sizes to accommodate different yarn weights.

1 Remove the strip that holds together the prongs of the hairpin. Knot the yarn around the left prong as shown with the knot at the center. Hold the ball of yarn in front of the right prong and return the joining strip to the prongs. Tape yarn end to the strip to hold the first loop in place.

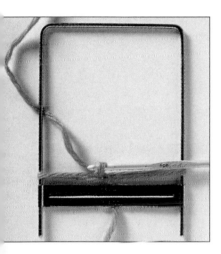

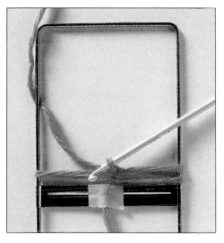

2 Pass the yarn behind the pin and insert hook under front of knotted loop (on left); yo and draw up loop; yo and draw through for ch, then work one sc.

3 Turn pin right to left; this will automatically wrap the yarn around the pin. Remove the hook and insert it under the front strand of the knot. Work another sc.

4 Repeat steps 2 and 3 until the piece is the desired length. Work last sc. Cut yarn and fasten off. For a long strip, when pin is filled, slide loops off prongs retaining only the last few loops to continue on.

5 Slide complete strip off prongs. Now you are ready to complete the decoration on the rings (or loops) at the edge.

Hairpin Lace

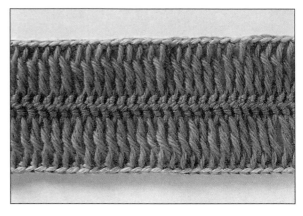

6 Make a slip knot on the hook. Leaving ring strands twisted as they came off the pin, insert the hook into the first ring along one edge, yo, and draw up loop (2 loops on hook). Yo and complete sc. Sc in each ring across edge. Fasten off.

7 Work other side to correspond. The sample above uses contrasting yarn to highlight the decoration. Naturally, you can use the same color yarn as for the rings if you prefer.

8 You can vary the edge to produce a zigzag as follows: * Leaving rings twisted, work (sc in next ring, ch 1) twelve times, then work 1 sc through all of the next 12 rings, drawing them together, ch 1 *; repeat from * to * along one edge. Fasten off. Work other side to correspond so the 12 drawn-together rings are opposite the 12 that are worked individually.

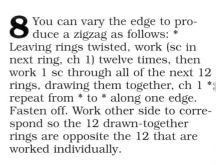

9 Strips of rings can be joined along the edges to form wider strips. Work a row of sc, following step 6 above, along a side of each strip. Then lay strips side by side to join the unfinished edges together with a slip stitch as follows: * Make slip knot on hook. With yarn held behind work, insert hook through next ring of lower strip then through next ring on top strip, yo, and draw through loop on hook to complete sl st *; repeat from * to * to join strips for entire length. Fasten off.

10 The joined strips appear compact, but made a soft fabric. You can join a number of strips to make a scarf or an afghan.

How to Work Corners in Filet Crochet

...ilet crochet is often used to make ...orders for tablecloths, napkins, or ...illow covers where squared corners ...re needed.

If the border is worked lengthwise ...) go all around the piece, the cor...ers must be planned for from the ...rst row (inner edge of border). ...easure the item to be edged and ...heck your gauge (see page 7) to ...etermine how many stitches you ...eed at each edge.

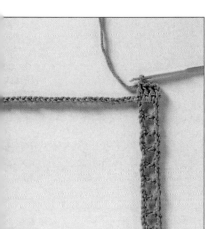

1 Corner with open squares: Make a chain long enough to fit the perimeter of the cloth. Mark the position for each corner. Work squares in open net stitch (see page 31) to first marked corner, work (dc, ch 5, dc) in same ch below (corner made), continue to work in open net stitch, working a corner at each marker. Join to first square but do not turn work.

2 To start new row, ch 5 for first open square, then work around, making an open square over each square and at corners work (dc, ch 5, dc) in 3rd ch of ch-5 below. See sample above.

 Corner with solid block: Work as for step 1 to first marked ...orner, dc in corner ch, then ch 3, ...otate work to work 2 dc over dc ...ist completed, dc in same corner ...i. Continue to work around as ...efore, making block at each corner ...arker.

4 On following rows, work corner block in top of corner ch-3 at each corner. See sample above.

5 Corner with double block: Work as before to marked corner ch, work 5 dc in this corner ch. At corners on following rows, work 5 dc in the third ch of the previous 5-dc group. See sample above.

The filet border can also be worked back and forth in rows (sideways) by working in sections, as described on the next page.

How to Work Corners in Filet Crochet

6 Open-square corner worked sideways: Make chain as long as desired width of border. Work back and forth until desired length of one side. On last row, * work to within 3 squares of end. * Ch 2 and work dc until there are 2 loops left on hook. Yo three times.

7 Work double treble (dtr) in next dc, leaving 3 loops on hook. Yo and draw through all loops to complete dtr and dc. * Ch 5, turn.

8 Work a row as normal. Work next row and end it by repeating from * to * (of steps 6 and 7). Repeat last 2 rows until only 2 squares remain. Ch 5, turn work.

9 *NOTE*: We used contrasting colored thread for greater visibility, but normally just continue with original color. Work as follows: Dc in next dc, ch 2, dc in center of next loop (lp) along slanted edge (lp formed by dtr or ch-5), ch 5, rotate work, and dc in same place as last dc, ch 2, sl st in next lp along slant, ch 2, rotate work, and dc in next lp.

10 * Ch 2, turn to work back to top edge. Ch 5, turn and work open squares, ending ch 2, sl st in next lp, ch 2, rotate piece to sl st in next lp *; repeat from * to * until you have completed corner. Work as usual to next corner. Continue to work border to last corner. Work last corner, ending with a filet crochet seam (see page 88) to complete.

Variations for Working Filet Crochet Corners

1 Alternating open and block squares, work 10 alternating block net squares (see page 31), beginning with a block square. Work for desired length to corner, leaving last row end with block square. * Ch 1, turn. Skip first dc, sl st in next 3 dc, ch 3, work 2 dc over next ch-2, dc in next dc *; complete row in pattern.

2 Ch 3, turn. Work in pattern, ending with block square above open square (leaving last block square unworked). Repeat from * to * (of step 1). Continue in this manner, beginning and ending rows as before, until only 2 squares remain. Now ch 2 and dc in last dc on previous row as shown.

3 Other half of corner (shown here in contrasting color for visibility): Rotate work as needed to work stitches into slanted edge. Ch 3 (for first dc), work 2 dc over the single dc made at the end of previous row, dc in top of last dc in row below, * ch 2, sl st in top of ch-3 below, ch 3, dc in top of ch-3 in following row.

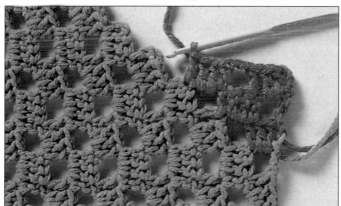

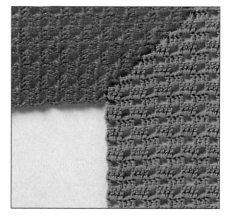

4 Turn work to work back to top edge over stitches just made. Work 2 dc over ch-2, dc in first dc of next block, ch 2, skip 2 dc, dc in top of ch-3. Ch 3, turn. Next row: Work 2 dc over ch-2, dc in next dc, ch 2, skip 2 dc, dc in next dc, 2 dc over ch-2, dc in top of dc where ch-2 just worked is anchored. *

5 Continue to work in this manner, working from * to * but adding extra open and block squares with succeeding rows, until you have completed corner and have same number of squares as for previous section of border. Now work as usual to next corner. Sample shows completed corner.

Variations for Working Filet Crochet Corners

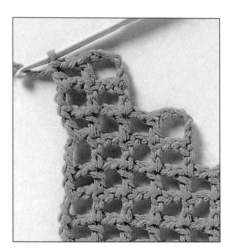

6 Open squares: Work in open net stitch, 8 squares wide, to corner, then form slanted edge with steps that are 2 stitches wide and 2 rows high as follows: At inner (slanted) edge, leave 2 squares unworked at end of row, then work next row as usual.

7 To work other half of corner (shown here in contrasting color), ch 5, and complete squares over the 2 remaining squares; then rotate work as needed to work stitches, ch 5, dc in same place as last dc was worked, ch 2, dc in top of dc at edge of row below, rotate work to work dc in dc below, ch 2, dc over ch-5.

8 Ch 2, turn. Work in pattern back to top edge. Ch 5, turn. Work in pattern, completing fourth square by working dc in top of edge dc of row below, rotate work to dc in dc below, ch 2, dc over ch-5 (inner corner worked).

9 Ch 2, turn. Work in pattern back to top. Ch 5, turn. Continue as before, completing 2 more squares for every 2 rows and working inner corner as before, until you work the last inner corner.

10 Ch 2, turn. Now work in pattern back to top edge. Ch 5, turn. Continue in pattern with 8 open spaces to next corner.

Working in Rounds Beyond Center Ring

After the completion of center ring (see pages 17–19), working in rounds can begin to change. You can make lacy motifs worked alone for centerpieces or joined to other motifs each made separately.

1 Centerpiece example: For center ring, ch 9 and join with sl st to form ring. **Rnd 1**: Ch 3 (counts as dc), work 31 more dc in ring. Join with sl st to top of ch-3. **Rnd 2**: Ch 3, then * ch 4, skip next dc, sc in next dc, ch 10, skip next dc, sc in next dc *.

2 Repeat from * to * six more times, then ch 4, skip 1 dc, sc in next dc, ch 5, double treble (dtr) in initial ch-1.

3 **Rnd 3**: Ch 3, work dc over same arch, * ch 4, work 5 dc over next ch-10 arch *; repeat from * to * around, ending with 3 dc in first arch to complete 5-dc group; sl st in top of ch-3. **Rnd 4**: Ch 3, work 2 dc in next dc, * ch 4, 2 dc in first dc of next 5-dc group, dc in next 3 dc, 2 dc in last dc of group *; repeat from * to * around, ending ch 4, 2 dc in next dc, dc in last 2 dc. Join with sl st to top of ch-3.

4 Continue to work around, working 2 dc in first and last dc of each dc group until each group has 13 dc. **Next rnd**: Begin to decrease 1 dc at each end of each group, leaving it unworked, on each rnd, and between each group work arches as follows: ch 7, sc over arch below, ch 7 (two 7-ch arches made). Continue to work around, decreasing on dc groups and adding another ch-7 arch between groups on following rnds, until there are 3 dc left in each group with 6 arches between. This is a sample of the completed centerpiece.

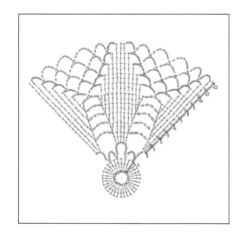

5 This is a scheme to follow for making this same centerpiece. See page 8 for the list of symbols.

Working in Rounds Beyond Center Ring

6 Make a motif, working the first 2 rnds as for centerpiece on previous page, ending Rnd 2 with ch 10 (in place of ch 5 and dtr) and join with sl st to initial ch-1. Cut yarn and fasten off.

7 Make another motif, ending Rnd 2 with ch 4 (in place of ch 10), then working a dc over an arch of the first motif (joining made), ch 4, then sl st in initial ch back in the second motif. Fasten off.

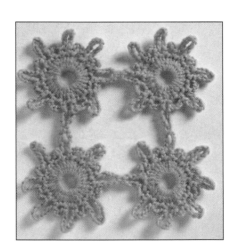

9 Make a center motif to fill in the open space as follows: Ch 8 and join with sl st to form a ring. Ch 1, work 16 sc in ring. Join with sl st to first sc.

8 Make two more motifs, joining each to form a square as shown, making joining to adjacent arch. (On fourth motif, you will be joining an arch to each of two previously made motifs.)

10 **Rnd 2**: Ch 1 (do not count a sc), * sc in first 3 sc, ch 1, s over adjacent ch-10 arch on large motif, ch 1, skip 1 sc on center mot *; repeat from * to * around, attach center motif to each large motif in turn. Sl st in last sc of center motif and fasten off. Sample shows completely joined motifs.

Hairpin Lace Designs:
Joining Strips and Embroidery

1 There are several ways to join hairpin lace strips. An easy way to join adjacent edges is to use a crochet hook to draw the tip of the first loop on the second side through the loop on the first side and then pick up the next loop on the first side to draw through the loop from the second side.

2 Continue to alternate sides until all loops are worked. Secure last loop with separate yarn and a yarn needle.

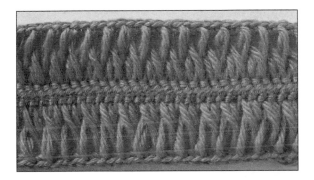

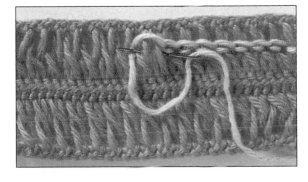

3 If you wish to insert a single strip of hairpin lace between two fabric pieces, finish each looped edge by working * sc through 2 loops at a time (with loops twisted only once), then ch 1*; repeat from * to * along one edge, then work other edge to match.

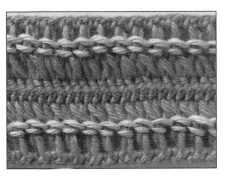

4 To decorate strip (with finished edges) with colored embroidery, use a yarn needle to embroider a row of chain stitch along one side of strip, working each chain stitch over a uniform number of strands—4, in this case.

5 Repeat along other side of hairpin lace strip. The sample shows a completed strip.

Hairpin Lace Designs:
Lacy Trims and Joining

7 Repeat from * to * for every 5 loops across the edge. At end of row, cut yarn and fasten off. Work trim along opposite edge. Work trim along one edge of second strip. Now add trim to remaining side and join it to the first strip as you work as follows: On first 5 loops, work 3 sc as before, * ch 2, sc over ch-5 arch of adjacent strip, ch 2 (joining made), then make 3 sc over same 5 loops, work 3 sc over next 5 loops *.

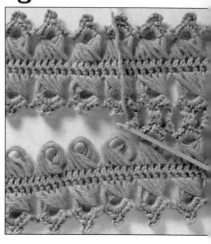

6 To trim and join strips, first make 2 strips of hairpin lace the same length. Trim: With loops twisted the same way throughout, * insert hook through 5 loops and work 3 sc over all 5 loops together, ch 5, work 3 more sc over same loops *.

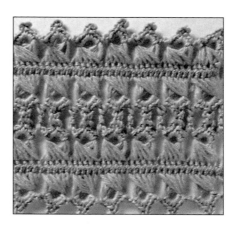

8 Repeat from * to * across, working back and forth to trim and join strips as you go, ending with joining, work 3 sc over last 5 loops. Fasten off. Sample shows completed piece.

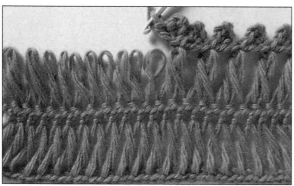

9 Lacy trim (suitable for a towel): Finish one edge of strip working (sc in one twisted edge loop, ch 1) across. On other edge, * insert hook through next 2 twisted loops to work sc, ch 3, sc in third ch from hook (picot made), hdc in last sc made over 2 loops *.

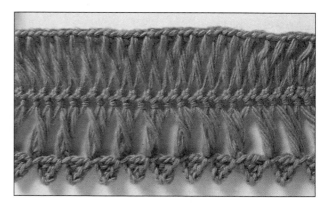

10 Repeat from * to * across, ending with sl st in last sc. Fasten off. Sample shows completed trim.

Lace Patterns: Clover Motif

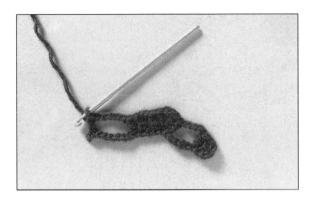

1 Ch 22. **Row 1**: Work dc in fourth ch from hook, dc in next dc, ch 5, skip 5 ch (on foundation ch), work (2 dc, ch 2, 2 dc) in next ch, ch 2, skip 2 ch, dc in next 2 ch, ch 6, skip 6 ch, dc in last ch. Do not turn work.

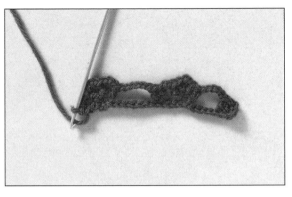

2 Work (ch 3 and dc) 3 times in same ch as last dc was worked (clover).

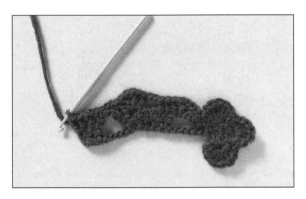

3 Ch 1, turn. **Row 2**: On each ch-3 of clover, work (sc, hdc, 3 dc, hdc, sc) for leaf, then ch 5, work 2 dc over ch-6, dc in next 2 dc, ch 2, work (2 dc, ch 2, 2 dc) over ch-2 between the two 2-dc group, ch 2, sc over ch-5, ch 2, dc in 2 dc, dc in top of turning ch. Ch 3, turn.

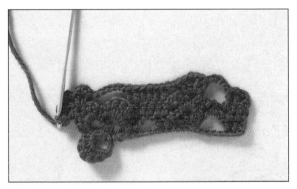

4 **Row 3**: Skip first dc (ch-3 counts as first dc), dc in next 2 dc, ch 5, work (2 dc, ch 2, 2 dc) over ch-2 between dc groups, ch 2, dc in next 4 dc, work 2 dc over ch-5, ch 6, work (dc and ch 3) three times in center dc of center leaf, then dc once more in same place (another clover).

5 Ch 1, turn. **Row 4**: In each ch-3 of clover, work (sc, hdc, 3 dc, hdc, sc) for leaf, ch 5, work 2 dc over ch-6, dc in next 6 dc, ch 2, work (2 dc, ch 2, 2 dc) over ch 2 between dc groups, ch 2, sc over ch-5, ch 2, dc in last 3 dc.

Lace Patterns: Clover Motif

6 Ch 3, turn. **Row 5**: Skip first dc, dc in next 2 dc, ch 5, work (2 dc, ch 2, 2 dc) over ch-2 between dc groups, ch 2, dc in next 8 dc, work 2 dc over ch-5, ch 6, work (dc and ch 3) three times in center dc of center leaf, then dc once more in same place (clover).

7 Ch 1, turn. **Row 6**: In each ch-3 of clover, work leaf as before (see Row 4), ch 5, work 2 dc over ch-6, dc in next 10 dc, ch 2, work (2 dc, ch 2, 2 dc) over ch-2 between dc groups, ch 2, sc over ch-5, ch 2, dc in last 3 dc.

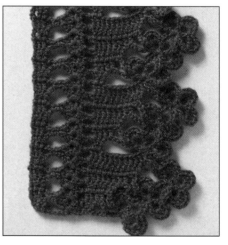

8 Ch 3, turn. **Row 7**: Skip first dc, dc in next 2 dc, ch 5, work (2 dc, ch 2, 2 dc) over ch-2 between dc groups, ch 2, dc in next 2 dc, ch 6, skip next 7 dc, in last dc before clover work (dc and ch 3) three times, dc in same dc again (clover).

9 Repeat Rows 2 through 8 for pattern for desired length. Fasten off.

10 The scheme to follow for this clover motif is shown to the right. See page 8 for the list of symbols.

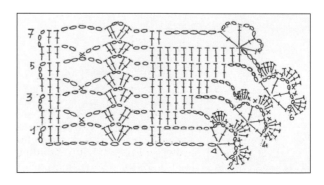

Belgian Lace

This lace pattern appears similar to lace made in Bruges, Belgium, but crocheting it is easy enough for a beginner to master.

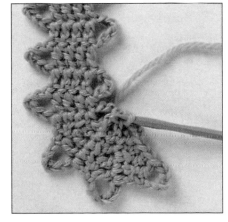

2 Dc in each of the remaining 3 ch (4 dc made). Chain 6, turn work.

1 Chain 10. Dc in seventh ch from hook.

3 Work dc in each dc. Chain 6, turn work. Repeat this step for desired length. In this way, you can make a simple strip to use as a trim.

4 You can also make a piece of serpentine lace. Work 10 rows as before, then begin curving as follows: Next row: Dc in 2 dc, hdc in next dc, sc in last dc. Ch 6, turn. Following row: Sc in sc, hdc in hdc, dc in 2 dc. Ch 6, turn.

5 Repeat these last 2 rows twice more. Next row: Dc in first 2 dc, hdc in hdc, sc in sc, ch 3, then insert hook through the 3 ch-6 arches worked after sc and work a sl st to draw them together. Ch 3, turn.

Belgian Lace

6 Next row: Sc in sc, hdc in hdc, dc in 2 dc (curve is made). Ch 6, turn.

7 Two dc, hdc, sc. Ch 3.

8 Yo and draw up loop in sl st (made to draw arches together in step 5); yo and draw through 2 loops but do not complete dc. Insert hook into next free arch and draw up loop; in one motion, draw it through to join the free arch and complete the dc.

9 Ch 3, turn. * Dc in 4 dc, ch 6, turn work, dc in 4 dc, ch 3, sl s in next free arch to join, ch 3, turn work *.

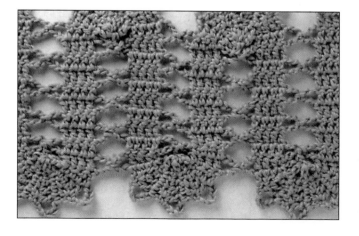

10 Repeat from * to * three more times. Then work curve as before (steps 4 through 6) and join new straight section to old (steps 7 through 10). Continue working in this manner for desired length, ending with step 10. Fasten off.

Increasing in Afghan (Tunisian) Stitch

Increase 1 stitch at right edge

1 Yarn over hook and draw up a loop in next vertical strand (3 loops of hook), then continue to draw up a loop in each vertical strand as usual.

2 On return row, work off loops as usual (see page 27), counting the added yo as a stitch.

Increase several stitches at right edge

3 At the end of the last return row, chain the desired number of stitches to be added.

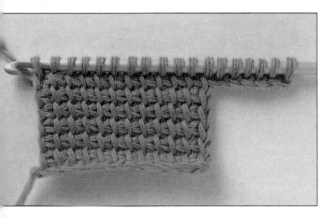

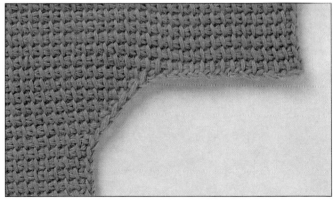

4 Draw up a loop in each chain as for a beginning row, then continue to draw up a loop in vertical strands to end of row. Work return row as usual on all stitches including added ones.

5 The sample above shows single increases repeated on several rows followed by a multiple increase. This type of increasing is useful for making jackets and other clothing.

Increasing in Afghan (Tunisian) Stitch

Increase 1 stitch at left edge

6 On the last return row *before* the planned increase row, work as follows: At the start of this return row, yo and draw through first loop on hook as usual, then ch 1 (increase will be worked on this ch on next row), complete return row as usual.

7 Next row: Draw up a loop in each vertical strand as usual until you reach the added ch; draw up a loop in this ch, then draw up a loop in last vertical strand. Work return row as usual.

Increase several stitches at left edge

8 Work across the increase row by drawing up a loop in each vertical strand as usual to end. With a separate piece of same yarn, chain the desired number of chains for increase, then draw up a loop in each ch to make the increase stitches.

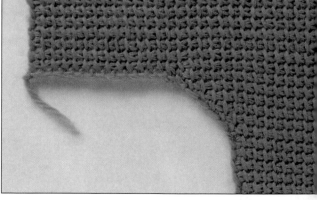

9 Starting with the added stitches, work the return row as usual.

10 Sample above shows single increases repeated on several rows followed by a multiple increase. This might be worked on the underarm of a garment.

Edgings Worked on Fabric

The size of the yarn should correspond to the weight of the fabric. If the fabric is lightweight, use a fine yarn. You may need to try several yarns or threads to find a suitable one. Once the yarn is matched to the fabric, you are ready to begin.

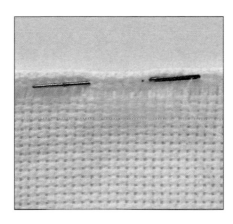

1 The first step is hemming the fabric (aida cloth is shown). If possible, remove a thread or two of the fabric to indicate a straight hemline on which you can work easily with a hook. Repeat for each edge of piece.

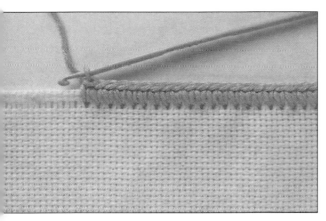

2 Insert hook into hemline to work sc around entire edge, working 3 or 4 sc at corners to turn. Join with sl st to first sc.

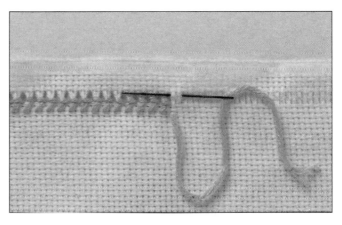

3 For a different hem, remove hemline threads as before. Embroider the lower hemline using a tapestry needle and yarn to work stitches as shown.

4 Folding over any excess fabric, finish this hem by crocheting sc around edge, working extra sc at corners and joining last sc to first with a sl st.

5 If the fabric you are trimming already has a double hemstitch in it (as shown), make a dc in each space of the hemstitch, working all around the piece and making extra dc to turn corners. Join with a sl st to first dc.

Edgings Worked on Fabric

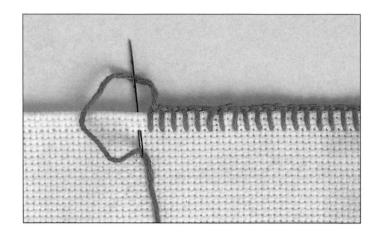

6 Instead of crocheting directly into the fabric, you can first establish a working edge by embroidering a row of blanket stitch all around the piece as shown. This works well for fabric on which removing a hemline thread is difficult.

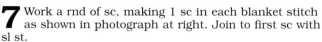

7 Work a rnd of sc, making 1 sc in each blanket stitch as shown in photograph at right. Join to first sc with sl st.

8 Work lace trim on the sc foundation as follows: Ch 5 (counts as first dc and ch), skip 2 sc, * dc in next dc, ch 2, skip 2 sc *; repeat from * to * around, working (dc, ch 5, dc) at corners. Join with sl st to third ch of initial ch-5.

9 Next rnd: Ch 1 and sc in first dc, * ch 8, skip 2 open spaces, sc in next dc *; repeat from * around, working (sc, ch 8, sc) in center ch of ch-5 at corners. Join with sl st to first sc.

10 Next row: Work (4 sc, ch 3, sl st in third ch from hook to make picot, 4 sc) over each ch-8 arch around. Join to first sc with sl st. Fasten off.

Irish Lace Motifs: Three-Layered Flower

In Irish lace, motifs, such as this flower, are worked separately. Completed motifs are arranged following a pattern, then joined together with an airy crocheted open or net-type stitch that allows the heavier motifs to stand out against the net background.

3 Make a slip knot on hook with next color (orange), then working on wrong side of yellow piece, insert hook under a center spoke and work sl st to join yarn, ch 6 (first dc and ch 3), work (dc and ch 3) on each remaining spoke around (8 orange spokes made). Sl st in 3rd ch of ch-6.

4 Ch 1, turn unit to right side with yellow on top. Folding yellow petals forward to work orange, work (sc, ch 1, 3 dc, ch 1, sc) over each ch-3 arch. Join to first sc. Fasten off.

With first color of yarn (yellow, in this case), ch 6. In the sixth ch from hook, work (dc and ch 2) seven times. Join with sl st to 3rd unworked ch of the initial chain (8 spokes made in wheel).

2 Ch 1, work (sc, ch 1, 2 dc, ch 1, sc) over each ch-2 arch around. Join with sl st to first sc. Fasten off.

5 With next color (pink), make slip knot and join, on wrong side, to an orange spoke, ch 7 (first dc and ch 4), work (dc and ch 4) on each remaining orange spoke. Join to 3rd ch of ch-7. Ch 1, and turn to right side to work (sc, ch 1, 4 dc, ch 1, sc) over each pink ch-4 arch. Join to first sc. Fasten off.

Irish Lace Motifs: Lancelot Leaf

7 Now add decorative details. First, work sl st through back loop only of each stitch around leaf to 3-sc group at tip, sl st in first of these sc, ch 2, skip center sc, sl st in 3rd sc, then sl st in each stitch to end. Ch 4 to add stem. Fasten off.

8 Another way to decorate leaf is to crochet sc worked through both loops of each stitch around, working 3 sc in center sc of 3-sc group and ending with 3 sc.

6 Ch 14. Sl st in second ch from hook, sc in next 3 ch, hdc in next 2 ch, dc in next 3 ch, 2 hdc in next 2 ch, sc in next ch, work 3 sc in last ch. Continue to work around other side of foundation chain, working sc in next ch, hdc in 2 ch, dc in 3 ch, hdc in 2 ch, sc in 3 ch, sl st in next ch. Ch 1.

9 Now work center ridge, making sl st at base of stitches (tip of leaf) with 1 stitch for each ch of foundation chain.

10 Chain 4 to form stem. Fasten off. Sample shows completed leaf.

Two-Color Jacquard Pattern in Single Crochet

Jacquard patterns produce a firmly textured piece suitable for place mats, pillow covers, or clothing where firmness is desired.

1 Chain the desired number of stitches for entire piece (multiple of 10 used, plus 1). Sc in desired number of stitches (5 shown) for first unit of first color (yellow, in this case), but do not complete last sc (2 loops on hook). Instead, draw through a loop of new color (blue) and complete sc (change colors this way throughout).

2 Hold old color (yellow) along chain and enclose it in stitches as you work forward. Then work desired number of sc for next unit (10 blue for pattern shown), but do not complete last sc (2 loops on hook).

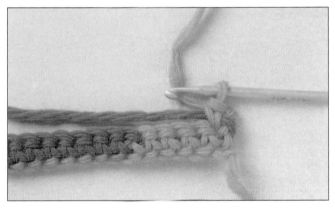

3 Draw through yellow to complete last st. Now work yellow sc, enclosing blue in stitches. Continue across row in this manner, alternating units of color and ending last unit with 5 sc. Ch 1 and turn, bringing unused color (blue) to front of work for wrong-side rows, then continue colors as established always enclosing unused color in work.

4 On following row (a right-side row), ch 1 and wrap unused color to back to enclose it in work. Continue work in colors as established.

5 This checkerboard pattern is worked in units of 10 stitches across and 9 rows in length. Alternate colors after every 9 rows to work blue above yellow and yellow above blue.

Two-Color Jacquard Pattern in Double Crochet

Using double crochet results in a somewhat softer piece than when using single crochet, but it also works well for place mats and clothing.

6 Chain the desired number of stitches (multiple of 16 shown, plus 3; in this example ch-3 was not counted as a stitch as it usually is). Work 5 dc in first color (pink), completing last dc only until 2 loops remain on hook. With new color (blue), draw through a loop to complete dc (change colors this way throughout).

7 Work dc with blue for next unit, enclosing pink in base of dc and changing colors on last dc as before.

8 Complete row, alternating units of color. Ch 3, turn, bring unused yarn to front (the wrong side of work) and catching it in first dc as shown. Work across row, keeping colors as established.

9 Complete row. Ch 3, turn, carrying unused yarn to back of work (wrong side), catching it in the first dc. Work row as usual.

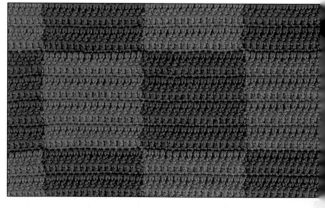

10 This checkerboard pattern is worked in square units 16 dc wide and 8 rows high. Alternate colors every 8 rows, working pink above blue and blue above pink.

Broomstick Lace

ven if today we use a very large
nitting needle or dowel (of up to an
ich in diameter) rather than an
ctual broomstick for this method,
is an unusual one. The resulting
ce is open but retains its form,
aking it suitable for baby blankets
r lacy sweaters. The larger the
ameter of knitting needle is, the
ore open the lace. Use a crochet
ook appropriate for the yarn being
sed.

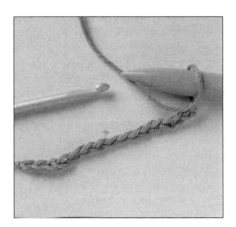

1 Chain the desired number of stitches (multiple of 4 as shown). Transfer the loop from crochet hook to knitting needle, enlarging it.

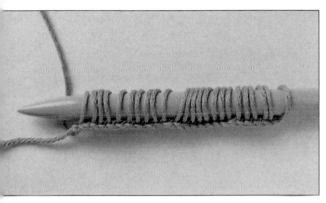

2 Use the crochet hook to draw up a loop in each ch of foundation chain and transfer it to the knitting nee-le as you go.

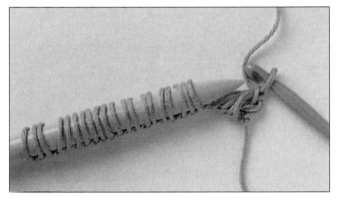

3 Hold the knitting needle in left hand. Insert crochet right to left through the first 4 loops on the needle and slide them off the needle. Yo and draw through all 4 loops at once; yo and draw through loop on hook to secure.

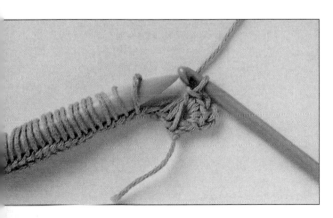

4 In the opening formed by hooking the loops together, work 4 sc, enclosing the top of the loops in the sc.

5 Continue in this manner to * hook next 4 loops together with sl st and work 4 sc in the space creat-ed *; repeat from * to * across row. Transfer the last loop left on hook onto the knitting needle.

Broomstick Lace

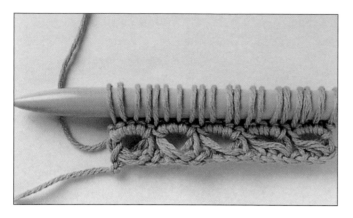

6 With crochet hook inserted through both top loops of sc, draw up a loop in each sc across row and transfer it to knitting needle as you go.

7 Turn work to work off loops as for steps 3 through 5. Note that the tops of the sc form a horizontal chain across work on this, the wrong side of work.

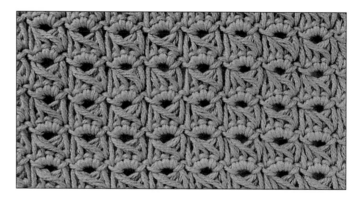

8 The completed pattern will have vertical columns of stitches.

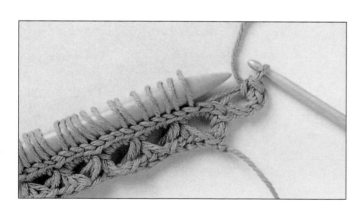

9 To vary the pattern, work the first row and pick up loops as usual. On the following row, hook only the first 2 loops and work 2 sc in them.

10 Then work 4 loops as usual across row, ending with a 2-loop stitch. Pick up a loop for each sc as usual. Alternate these 2 rows to produce the pattern shown above.

Woven Pattern on Net Stitch

Crocheting chains over a net background is an easy way to work vertical stripes and make plaid designs without using more than one color on a row as you crochet. The worked piece is firmer than the basic net piece, making it useful for place mats and afghans.

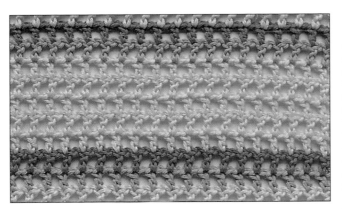

1 To prepare basic net piece, chain desired length. Work dc in fifth ch from hook (counts as first dc and ch 1), * ch 1, skip 1 ch, dc in next ch *; repeat from * to * across to end. Ch 5, turn. Work (dc in dc, ch 1) across, ending dc in third ch of turning ch. Ch 5, turn. Repeat this last row for desired length (allowing for some tightening when stripes are added) and work color rows as desired for horizontal stripes (pattern of 5 yellow rows, 1 turquoise, 1 blue is shown). Fasten off.

2 Make a slip knot and place on hook. Hold yarn behind work with left hand and draw through a chain in first square at left edge of first row. Insert hook in next square directly above and draw through another chain stitch. Work loosely enough to keep work flat.

3 Repeat, always making chain directly above previous one, up to top edge. Fasten off.

4 Alternate colors (as shown, 5 rows yellow, 1 turquoise, 1 blue) to correspond to horizontal pattern to make plaid. Sample shows front of completed plaid piece.

5 Sample shows the wrong side of the work, also with the plaid design. Weave in yarn ends with a yarn needle so work is both reversible and neat.

Woven Pattern on Net Stitch

6 This version of a two-color woven pattern with its jaunty stripes is a little more compact. On foundation chain, hdc in fourth ch from hook, then repeat (ch 1, skip 1 ch, hdc in next ch) across. Ch 3, turn. Continue working (hdc in hdc, ch 1) to form net. Work vertical chains in each opening as before but at end of each stripe, ch 2, and work back in opposite direction for next stripe. Sample shows front of work.

7 Sample shows the back, or wrong side, of work. Because one color is used for the net and one for the chain stripes, it is easier and faster to work.

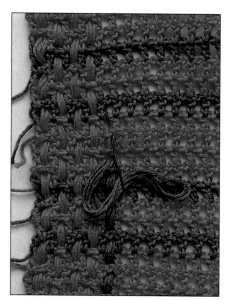

9 Use 4 strands of yarn per stripe, cutting it long enough to work entire stripe. Thread strands into yarn needle (with a blunt tip) and weave in and out of each opening, starting at bottom and working to top. Alternate colors for stripes same as for rows; also alternate the ins and outs of weaving for each vertical row.

8 Work on a base of net (see previous page), with a color pattern of 4 rows of orange, 1 blue, 2 orange, 1 blue. Instead of crocheted chains, the vertical stripes are worked by using a yarn needle to weave yarn strands.

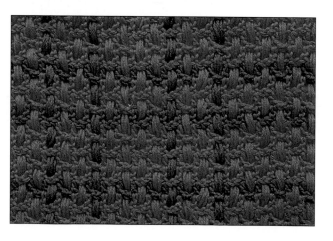

10 Secure yarn ends and weave them in neatly on back. Sample shows front of completed piece, which is reversible if neatly finished.

Irish Lace Motifs: Star Flower

1 Ch 4, working first ch loosely.
Rnd 1: In this first ch (fourth ch from hook), work 15 dc; join with sl st to top of initial ch (which counts as first of 16 dc).

2 **Rnd 2**: Ch 4, skip first dc, repeat (sc in next dc, ch 3, skip 1 dc) seven times, ending with sl st in first ch of ch-4.

3 **Rnd 3**: Ch 7, * reaching behind Rnd 2, yarn over, and insert hook from back to front around next sc with tip emerging again behind work; draw through a loop and work dc.

4 Ch 4 *; repeat from * to * six more times, join with sl st in third ch of ch-7. The ch-3 arches of Rnd 2 are left unworked and there are 8 ch-4 arches on Rnd 3.

5 **Rnd 4**: * To work point, ch 9, sl st in third ch from hook, sc in next ch, hdc in next ch, dc in next ch, tr in next 3 ch (point made), sl st in next dc of Rnd 3 *.

Irish Lace Motifs: Star Flower

6 Repeat from * to * seven more times; join with sl st to first ch of ch-9. Fasten off.

7 You can use the star flower as it is, or add a corolla for trim, working it in a lighter shade of yarn. Work as follows: Make a slip knot on hook, insert hook under an unworked ch-3 arch of Rnd 2, and attach yarn with a ch. * Working over ch-3 arch, work sc, ch 1, 3 dc, ch 1, sc *.

8 Repeat from * to * seven more times. Join with sl st to beginning ch. Fasten off. Sample shows completed star flower with corolla.

9 Variation of star flower: The petals are worked with afghan stitch (see page 27). Work first 2 rnds the same as for regular star flower (see previous page). **Rnd 3 (petal rnd):** * Ch 8, draw up loop second ch from hook and in each remaining ch, retaining all loops on hook, draw up another loop over ch-3 arch. Return row: Yo and draw through first 3 loops on hook, then work (yo, draw through next 2 loops) until 1 loop remains. Now draw up a loop in second and each remaining vertical strand (6 loops on hook), draw up loop over ch-3 arch. Work return row as before. Draw up loops through vertical strands and over arch ch as before (5 loops). Work return row. Draw up loop through vertical strand and over arch ch (3 loops); yo over and draw through all three loops. Work sc over same arch (petal made) *.

10 Repeat from * to * seven more times. Join to first ch with sl st. Fasten off. Sample above shows completed star flower with petals worked in afghan stitch.

Working Squares in Rounds

There are many ways to make a square beginning from the center. We have already seen some on pages 20 and 36. Here is another one worked in a checkerboard pattern of blocks and squares.

Square with block corners

1 Chain 8 and join with a sl st to form a ring. **Rnd 1**: Ch 7, dc in same ch as ring joining, * ch 1, skip 1 ch on ring, work (dc, ch 4, dc) in next ch *; repeat from * to * twice more. Join with sl st to 3rd ch of ch-7.

2 **Rnd 2**: Ch 4, * work 5 dc in 2nd ch of corner ch-4.

3 Ch 1, dc in dc, dc over next ch, dc in next dc (block made), ch 1 *; repeat from * to * twice more, then work 5 dc in 2nd ch of last corner ch-4, ch 1, dc in next dc, dc in ch. Join with sl st to 3rd ch of ch-4.

5 Ch 1, skip 1 dc, dc in last dc of 5-dc group, dc over ch-1, dc in dc, ch 1, skip 1 dc, dc in next dc, dc over ch-1 *; repeat from * to * twice more, then dc in first dc of corner group, ch 1, skip 1 dc, work 5 dc in center dc of group, ch 1, skip 1 dc, dc in last dc of group, dc over ch-1, dc in dc, ch 1. Join with sl st to top of ch-3. Continue to work rnds in this manner, alternating blocks with open spaces and adding a block to each side on each row, until square is the desired size.

4 **Rnd 3**: Ch 3, dc over ch 1 below, * dc in first dc of 5-dc group, ch 1, skip 1 dc, work 5 dc in next dc (center dc of 5-dc group).

Working Squares in Rounds

Variation of square with block corners

6 Ch 7. Work dc in fifth ch from hook, dc in last 2 ch of ch-7 (block made). **Rnd 1**: Ch 5, work dc in fourth ch from hook. Dc in next ch, dc in top of adjacent dc (last dc of first block), ch 2, dc in first ch of ch-7 (at base of same dc at end of block).

7 Continue working Rnd 1 around first block as follows: Ch 3, rotate piece to work next side, work 2 dc over post of dc just made, dc again in first ch of ch-7 to complete block, ch 2, skip next 2 ch (working below first block), dc in next ch, ch 3, rotate work, work 2 dc over post of dc just made, dc in same ch (base of ch-3) to complete block, ch 2, skip 2 ch, dc in next ch, ch 3, rotate work, work 2 dc over post of dc just made, dc in ch at base of dc to complete block, ch 2. Join with sl st to ch at base of first block of Rnd 1.

8 Continue to work around in this manner, working corners as before and adding a block to each side on every rnd. Alternate blocks and open spaces, working rnds until square is desired size. Fasten off.

Checkerboard square with open-square corners

9 Ch 12. Join to first ch with sl st to form ring. **Rnd 1**: Ch 5, skip next 2 ch of ring * work (dc, ch 5, dc) in next ch (corner made), ch 2, skip 2 ch *; repeat from * to * twice more, then dc in beginning ch at base of ch-5, ch 5. Join with sl st to third ch of beginning ch to complete last corner. **Rnd 2**: Ch 5, * skip ch-2, dc in next dc, work 2 dc over corner ch-5, work (dc, ch 5, dc) in center ch of same ch-5, work 2 more dc over same ch-5, dc in next dc, ch 2 *.

10 Repeat from * to * around, ending last repeat with corner and 2 dc over ch-5. Join with sl st to third ch of initial ch-5. Continue in this manner, working corners as before and adding a block to each side every rnd. Alternate block and open squares, working rnds until square is desired size. Fasten off.

Fur Stitch

This looped fur stitch is good for rugs, toy animals, and trim on garments. One method uses a large knitting needle (or dowel) to achieve loops of uniform length. The larger the needle is, the larger the loop will be. The other method does not require anything but a regular hook.

Fur stitch worked with knitting needle

1 Make a chain the desired length. **Row 1**: Work a row of sc across chain. Ch 1, turn work. **Row 2**: * Holding knitting needle parallel to work, wrap yarn from front to back over the needle.

2 With the hook, catch the yarn below the knitting needle and draw it through the loop on the crochet hook. Now there is 1 loop on hook and 1 on needle.

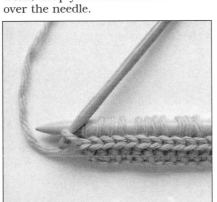

3 Sc in next sc *; repeat from * to * across row. At the end there will be as many loops on the hook as there were sc worked.

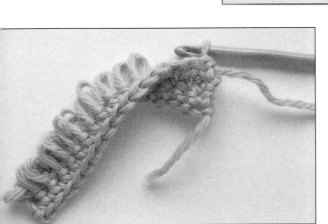

4 Unthread loops from knitting needle. Ch 1, turn. **Row 3**: Sc in each stitch across. Ch 1, turn.

5 Repeat Rows 2 and 3 until piece is desired length. Fasten off. Sample shows completed fur stitch.

Fur Stitch

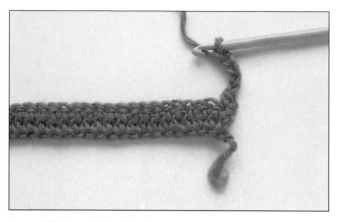

Fur stitch with chains

6 Make a chain of desired length. **Row 1**: Dc in fourth ch from hook, then dc in each ch of chain. Ch 1, turn. **Row 2**: Sc in front strand only (not in both top strands as usual) of first dc below, * ch 5, sc in front strand (also called loop) of next dc *.

7 Repeat from * to * across ending with last sc in top o ch-3. Ch 3 (counts as first dc of Row 3).

8 Turn work. **Row 3**: Folding Row 2 back out of the way, skip ch-3 below first sc, then work a dc in the unworked top strand of each remaining stitch of Row 1.

9 Ch 1, turn. Repeat Rows 2 and 3 for fur stitch pattern, working desired number of rows. Fasten off. Sample shows front of fur stitch.

10 Sample shows the wrong side of fur stitch with only dc rows visible.

Buttonholes

Horizontal buttonhole in single crochet

Work piece up to position for first buttonhole. Work buttonhole row to within 8 sc of edge as usual, then ch 5, skip 5 sc, sc in remaining 3 sc.

2 Ch 1, turn work. Work first 3 sc, work 5 sc over ch-5 arch, then continue as usual.

3 Sample shows piece with completed buttonhole.

Vertical buttonhole in single crochet

4 Work to end of row on which the buttonhole begins. * Ch 1, turn, sc in 3 sc *; repeat for 5 rows, leaving other section unworked. Fasten off when fifth row is completed.

5 Turn work to work remaining section. Skip 1 sc on last completed row for buttonhole opening and begin in next sc by inserting hook to draw up a loop and ch 1.

Buttonholes

6 Then work in sc to complete 5 rows on the second section. Next row: Sc to buttonhole opening, ch 1, sc in last 3 sc at edge. On the following row, sc across, working sc over ch-1 at buttonhole. Continue as usual.

7 Sample shows completed vertical buttonhole.

Horizontal buttonhole in double crochet

8 Complete last row before start of buttonhole. Buttonhole row: Work first 3 dc, then reach back with hook to draw up a loop around post of dc just worked. Yo and draw through both loops on hook (sc made).

9 * Draw up a loop through strand at lower left edge of sc just made, yo and complete sc *; repeat from * to * until you have added a total of 5 stitches. Skip 5 dc below, then continue to work as usual across row.

10 Sample shows completed buttonhole in dc.

Wrapped Stitches

These stitches are very compact. While they can be used for an entire (but heavy) piece, they also can be used for attractive edgings. Making them requires a lot of yarn, so you need to purchase extra yarn for working these patterns.

Column stitches

1 Make a chain the desired length, allowing 5 ch for turning. **Row 1**: * Yarn over (yo) six times, then insert hook in sixth ch from hook and draw up a loop (8 loops on hook).

2 Yo again and carefully draw through all 8 loops on hook *.

3 Repeat from * to *, working a wrapped stitch in each ch across. Ch 1, turn.

4 **Row 2**: Work sc in each wrapped stitch across, sc in top of turning ch. Ch 5, turn.

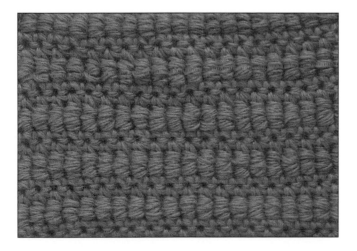

5 **Row 3**: Skip first sc, work a wrapped stitch in each remaining sc across. Ch 1, turn. Repeat Rows 2 and 3 for pattern. Sample shows completed pattern with column stitches.

Wrapped Stitches

6 Sample shows wrong side of column stitch pattern described on previous page.

Variation of column stitch

7 Make foundation chain. **Row 1**: Yo three times and draw up loop in fourth ch from hook (5 loops on hook). Yo again and draw through all 5 loops on hook; * yo three times, draw up loop in next ch; yo and draw through all 5 loops on hook *; repeat from * to * across. Ch 3, turn. **Row 2**: Skip first stitch, work wrapped stitch as before in each remaining stitch. Ch 3, turn. Repeat Row 2 for pattern. Sample shows completed pattern.

Cluster stitch

8 Make a foundation ch with an even number of ch. **Row 1**: Skip first 4 ch (counting from hook), * work (yo and draw up loop) three times in next ch (7 loops on hook).

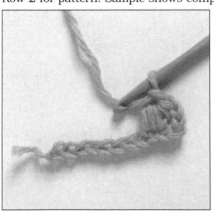

9 Yo again and draw through all 7 loops on hook (cluster made), ch 1.

10 Skip next ch *; repeat from * to * across row ending with dc in last ch. Ch 3, turn. **Row 2**: Work (cluster, ch 1) each in ch-1 worked after clusters on previous row, ending with dc in top of turning ch. Ch 3, turn. Repeat Row 2. Sample on right shows completed cluster stitch pattern.

Joining Squares

Single squares can be joined together in many ways besides simply sewing them together on the wrong side with a sewn slipstitch. Below are two easy ways to crochet the squares together. We used a contrasting colored yarn for the joinings for greater visibility.

1 Make the desired number of squares, remembering that the joinings will add to the overall dimensions of your project. Work a row of single crochet around each square and fasten off. As you assemble squares, be sure the right side (front) of each square faces the same way.

Simple joining

2 Attach yarn to a corner of one square with a ch 1. Sc in first sc on first square (A), * skip 1 sc on second square (B), sc in next sc on B, skip 1 sc on A, sc in next sc on A *.

3 Repeat from * to * along entire side of adjoining squares. Join squares in strips, then join strips, matching corners, to form afghan or other project.

Lacy variation of simple joining

4 Attach yarn with ch-1 in corner of one square. Sc in first sc of first square (A), * ch 1, skip 1 sc on second square (B), sc in next sc on B, ch 1, skip 1 sc on A, sc in next sc on A *.

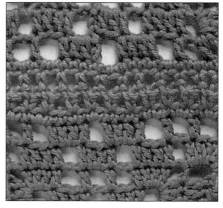

5 Repeat from * to * along the sides of the squares, joining squares in strips, then joining strips.

Joining Squares

Wide lacy joining

6 Add a second row to square before joining, working as follows: Along side edges, repeat (sc in sc, ch 5, skip 2 sc) and, at corners, work ch 9 without skipping any sc.

7 Work all around first square in this manner, ending row with a sl st in first sc of row.

9 Work edging on 3 sides of third square, then join it to the second square along one side to the fourth (inner) corner. At corner, ch 4, sc at joining of ch-9 loops for previous squares, ch 4. Join with sl st to first sc on third square.

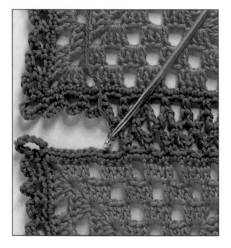

8 On next square (B), work around 3 sides of square as before, ending at corner. Now join to previous square (A) as follows: At corner, ch 4, sc over ch-9 loop on adjoining corner on A, ch 4, * sc in next sc on B, ch 2, sc over adjoining ch-5 loop on A, ch 2, skip 2 sc on B *; repeat from * to * along edge, joining corner loops as before.

10 Work edging on 2 sides of fourth square (shown at lower right in photograph). Then join next edge to third square, working to corner at center; ch 4, sc in joining of 3 other squares; ch 4, work joinings to adjacent square along fourth edge, joining as before to loops; and at last corner ending with final ch 4. Join with sl st to first sc. Continue to join squares in this manner. You can also join squares in strips, then join strips, working side edges and joining at corners to correspond.

Irish Lace Motifs: Eight-Petal Flower

This basic Irish lace motif can also be used alone to trim ~~a~~ blouse or even to cover a threadbare spot or stain on a sweater!

1 Chain 9. Join to first ch with a sl st to form a ring. Ch 1 and work 16 sc in ring; join with sl st to first ~~sc~~. Make first petal: Sl st on next sc, ch 16, then sc in second ch from hook, hdc in next ch, dc in next ch, treble (tr) in next 7 ch.

2 Dc in next 2 ch, hdc in next ch, sc in next ch, then sl st in next sc of circle.

3 Ch 1, turn work. In each stitch of petal work sc to tip, work (sc, ch 1, sc) over ch at tip, then continue on other side of petal working sc in each ch back to base of petal, ending with sl st in last ch.

4 Ch 1, turn. Working in back loop only of each sc, sc in each sc to tip of petal, work (sc, ch 1, sc) over ch at tip, sc in back loop of each sc to base of petal.

5 Work sl st in next sc on circle. Now ch 16, then working as for first petal, work sc in second ch from hook, then work hdc, dc, 7 tr, 2 dc, hdc, and sc.

Irish Lace Motifs: Eight-Petal Flower

6 Sl st in next sc of circle. Now repeat step 3. Ch 1, turn. Then with wrong sides of petals held together, insert hook through back loop only of sc on second petal (new petal) and back loop of corresponding sc on first petal (previous petal) and sc in first 7 sc, joining them together.

7 Then continue on just the new petal, working sc in back loop only of each sc around petal and working (sc, ch 1, sc) over ch-1 at tip.

8 Work 6 more petals in same manner to the last 7 sc on the last petal. Then work the last 7 sc, joining the last petal to the free side of the first petal.

9 Cut yarn and fasten off. The flower is completed!

10 The scheme can help you visualize the different steps of the piece.

Braided Stitch

This stitch produces an open work that is useful for curtains, garments, or a lacy afghan that is not too frilly. A single row of the stitch can serve as the center of an insert on a tablecloth or used as a joining.

1 Make a foundation chain with a multiple of 4, plus 1. Work dc in fifth ch from hook, ch 3, then make a dc into top of dc just completed (first X made).

2 * Ch 1, skip next ch of foundation ch, in next ch work treble (tr), leaving last 3 loops on hook.

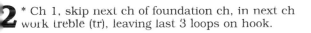

3 Skip next ch, yo, and draw up a loop in next stitch (5 loops on hook). Yo and draw through 2 loops. Repeat (yo and draw through 2 loops) until only 1 loop remains on hook (joined tr and dc made).

4 Ch 1, work another dc by inserting hook into the joining of dc and tr just made (another X made) *.

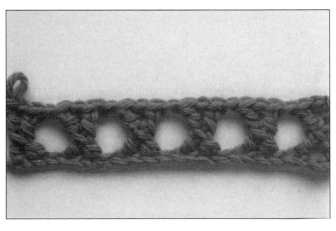

5 Repeat from * to * across foundation chain, making a row of braided X's.

Braided Stitch

6 Ch 3, turn work. Dc in second leg at top of X below, ch 4, and dc where ch-3 and dc join (first X on row formed). Now continue as before to work rows of braided stitch, working each new X above X on previous row, to make a lacy pattern as shown on left.

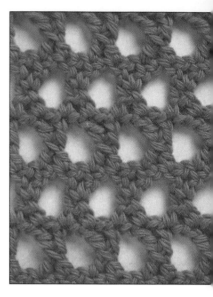

8 Yo and draw through first 2 loops on hook, then starting from step 3, continue to work X's across row, ending with ch 1, tr in last stitch of row. This produces a diagonal or alternating X pattern as shown.

7 Variation of braided stitch: At the beginning of every second row, ch 5, yo twice, and insert hook into third stitch (last stitch of X below) and draw up a loop (4 loops on hook).

9 You can add an edging to a single row of pattern, working a row of sc across top edge, then working a row of reverse single crochet (see page 37).

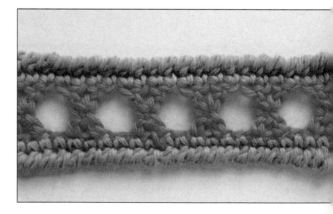

10 Repeat sc and reverse sc rows along opposite edge (edges here are shown in blue for visibility). Use for an insert or trim.

Cords

Crocheted cords can be used as ties or belts as well as for decorations and trims on crocheted or fabric garments and on household items.

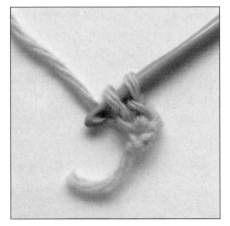

Simple cord

1 Ch 2. Sc in second ch, then * insert hook through the loop at lower left side of sc just made and draw up a loop.

2 Yo and draw through both loops on hook to complete sc *.

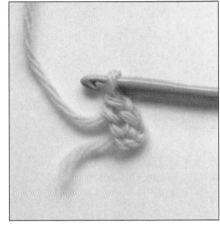

3 Repeat from * to * until cord is desired length.

Round cord

4 Ch 5. Join with sl st to form a ring. Ch 1, sc in next ch.

5 Continue to work sc in each ch around. Then continue to work sc in sc around and around until cord is desired length. Cut yarn, leaving an end. Thread end into yarn needle and catching loop of each unworked sc with needle; draw end stitches tightly together and fasten off. This cord is good for belts.

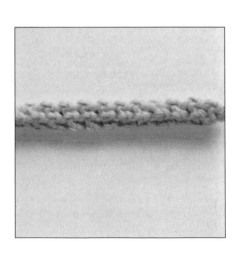

Cords

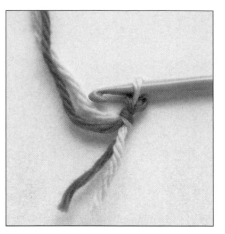

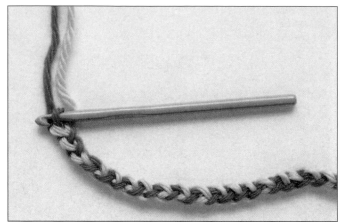

7 Now contin-ue to make chains, alternat-ing colors A and B as you work each stitch until cord is desired length. Fasten off both colors.

Simple chain cord with 2 colors

6 Work with 2 strands of yarn, each a different color, holding them together as one to ch 1. Draw loop of 1 color (A) through the loop of the other color (B) to make next ch. One loop remains on hook.

Cord worked with 3 colors

8 Working in same manner as for 2-color cord, hold 3 color strands together to ch 1. Draw color A and B loops through color C, then continue to make chains, 1 color at a time and change color with each ch, rotat-ing the 3 colors as you work stitches until cord is desired length.

9 These multicolored cords can be used for trim as shown. Simply fasten a safety pin to one end and use it as a guide to weave the cord in and out of the edge stitches (a row of tr is worked at edge makes the weaving easy).

Doubled chain cord with 2 colors

10 For a thicker and more solid cord, use 2 strands of 2 different colors and work as for steps 6 and 7, alternating colors, but always using 2 strands for each color.

Seams

Seams are used to join crocheted pieces of a garment or to join sections of a household item, such as units for an afghan. For pieces made of wool, you may wish to block the pieces first, carefully following the instructions on the yarn label. Synthetic yarns usually don't need blocking and should not be ironed.

Backstitch

1 Use for pieces with irregular edges, such as sleeve seam. Thread matching yarn in yarn needle (contrasting color shown for visibility). With right side (front) of pieces together, attach yarn and work backstitch (stitch back to last stitch, then bring yarn up ahead of stitch being worked). Make seam 1 or 2 stitches in from edge.

Slip stitch

2 Use for piece with irregular edges. With right sides together, work near edge; inserting hook through both pieces to catch yarn held below, draw up a loop and in a continuous motion draw it on through loop on hook. Repeat for seam.

Sewn chain stitch

3 This duplicates crocheted slip stitch in step 2, but is sewn with yarn needle. Insert needle into previous chain loop and bring it up a short distance ahead, catching yarn for new stitch under needle as shown. Draw yarn through to complete chain.

Single crochet

4 Use for straight edges. Sc can be worked on right side (front of work) if you want to highlight the seam. With right sides together for concealed seam, wrong sides together for visible seam, work a row of sc along edge, spacing stitches to keep work flat without stretching or drawing in edges.

Single crochet and chain

5 Use for thick yarn or where elasticity is desired. With right sides together, work sc and ch 1, or sc and ch 2, as desired along edge, skipping a tiny space after each sc to allow for chains and ending with sc.

Seams

Weaving with needle

6 Use for straight edges, laying seam edges side by side, right-side up. Stitch, inserting needle under 1 crochet stitch (for sc) or half a stitch (for dc) on one side, then under next stitch (or half stitch) on other side and draw sides together. Work back and forth, sewing under corresponding stitch on first side, then next stitch on other side, weaving sides together.

Alternating slip stitch

7 Lay seam edges side by side. Work sl st at lower edge of right-hand piece by inserting hook front to back through first row to make sl st. Then sl st in corresponding place on other piece. Continue to work sl st for seam, alternating from side to side for each stitch.

Sewing upper edges

8 Use to join top edges of stitches, as for shoulder seam. Lay pieces flat with top (final) edges butting and with right sides facing up. Draw needle through 1 loop (closest to seam) of chain at top of first stitch, then through 1 loop (closest to seam) of corresponding stitch on other piece. Sew through next stitch on same side and return to first side. Weave back and forth in this manner.

Seam for filet crochet

9 Lay work right-side up with seam edges side by side. Draw through a loop in first stitch, ch 2. Yo, insert hook in corresponding stitch on other side and work dc, * ch 2, yo and draw up loop in next stitch on first side (always work into corners of open squares), yo and draw through first 2 loops on hook, then yo and draw up loop on corresponding stitch on other side, yo and draw through 2 loops (3 loops remain on hook). (Yo and draw through 2 loops) twice to complete stitches. *

10 Repeat from * to * along seam edges. Sample shows completed seam.

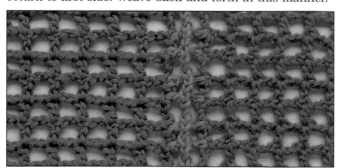

Rickrack Trim

Rickrack can be used to add color and interest (as well as to save time) when you incorporate lacy edgings into your crocheting. It works well for trimming towels, tablecloths, and other household items. Use a fine crochet thread and small hook.

Simple border

1 Insert hook into a high point on rickrack, near but not right at edge, and draw up loop to ch 1. Work sc at this "peak" of zigzag, * ch 3, dc at next "valley," ch 3, sc at next peak *. Repeat from * to * across length on rickrack.

2 Ch 4, turn. Next row: Skip first stitch below, dc in center ch of ch-3, * ch 1, dc in next stitch, ch 1, dc in center ch of next ch-3. Repeat from * to * across. Ch , turn. Work a row of sc, working in each dc and over each ch-1 across. Fasten off.

3 Rotate rickrack to trim other side. Attach thread to first peak and * ch 8.

4 * Yo three times, insert hook in eighth ch from hook and work double treble (dtr), leaving 3 loops on hook; yo twice and work treble (tr), leaving 2 additional loops on hook (5 in all); yo and dc, leaving 2 more (now 7) loops on hook.

5 Yo and, in one motion, draw through all loops on hook to complete scallop, then ch 1, sc in next peak *; repeat from * to * across rickrack.

Rickrack Trim

Fringed edging

6 Attach thread at peak of rick-rack, ch 5. * Yo twice, insert hook into rickrack half way down to "valley," work treble (tr) until 2 loops remain on hook; yo twice, insert hook into rickrack half way up to next peak, and draw up a loop (5 loops on hook); yo and draw through 2 loops at a time until 3 loops remain; yo and draw through all 3 loops (joint tr worked), ch 3, hdc at peak, ch 3 *; repeat from * to * across length of rickrack. Fasten off.

7 Next row: Attach thread to second ch at start of last row. Ch 1, * work 2 sc over ch-3 arch, sc in next stitch, ch 3, sc in first ch of ch 3 just made (picot made) *; repeat from * to * across. Fasten off.

8 Rotate work to trim other side of rickrack. Attach thread half way down to valley, ch 2, work dc half way up to next peak, * ch 2, work (dc, ch 5, dc) at top of peak, ch 2; half way down to valley, work dc, leaving 2 loops on hook; half way to peak, work dc, leaving its last 2 loops on hook; yo and draw through all loops on hook (joined dc worked) *; repeat from * to * across. Fasten off.

9 Attach thread at first dc of previous row and ch 5, * work (dc, ch 5, dc) in center ch of next ch-5, ch 2, work joined dc as follows: work first leg in last dc of last peak, skip joined dc, and work second leg in first dc of next peak, then complete joined dc, ch 2 *; repeat from * to * across. Fasten off. Repeat this last row one or more times as desired.

10 For each fringe, cut four 5-inch strands of thread. Hold strands together and fold in half. Insert hook (back to front) through ch-5 arch at edge to catch folded loops, draw looped end through arch, then bring fringe ends down through the loop; pull ends to tighten knot. Make fringe in each ch-5 arch at edge. With scissors, trim fringe ends to an even length.

Crocheted Inserts

This insert can be worked fairly quickly to be put between two pieces of fabric for a tablecloth or elegant place mat. We show here a basic pattern that can be varied as you wish. However, be sure that there are picots at regular intervals so you can attach the insert to the fabric.

1 Ch 12 and join with sl st to form a ring. Ch 1, work 12 sc in ring, ch 12.

2 Turn work. Counting back from base of ch-12 just made, sl st in fourth sc. Turn work and make 5 sc over ch-12 just made, ch 7. Turn work and sl st in the third sc on the beginning ring.

3 Ch 1, turn work. Work 5 sc over ch-7, work ch 3, sl st in third ch from hook (picot made), work 5 more sc over same ch-7. * Continuing on around edge, work 7 sc over ch-12, ch 12.

4 Turn work and sl st in fourth sc below. Turn work. Ch 1, work 12 sc over ch-12 arch just made, ch 12. Turn work. Sl st in fourth sc below.

5 Ch 1, turn work. Work 5 sc over ch-12 arch just made, ch 7. Turn work, sl st in fourth sc of 12 sc worked over previous arch.

Crocheted Inserts

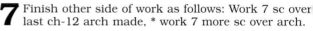

6 Ch 1, turn work. Work 5 sc over ch-7, make picot as before, 5 sc over same ch-7 *; repeat from * to * for desired length.

7 Finish other side of work as follows: Work 7 sc over last ch-12 arch made, * work 7 more sc over arch.

8 Work 4 sc in next adjoining arch, ch 7. Turn work. Sl st in fifth sc from last of those just worked in previous arch. Ch 1, turn work. Work (5 sc, picot, 5 sc) over ch-7 just made, then make 3 more sc in arch below (where 4 sc were already worked) *.

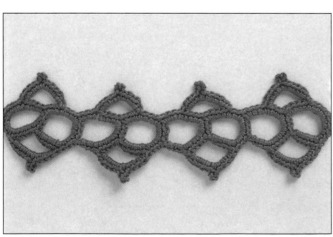

9 Repeat from * to * until piece is complete. Fasten off.

10 Carefully press piece (if thread label permits). Fold under and baste fabric edges. Join to fabric edges as shown, embroidering the fabric edges with blanket stitch and attaching the crocheted insert at picots.

Sunburst Pattern in Two Colors

Make a foundation chain with a multiple of 6, plus 5. **Row 1**: With color A (orange, in this case), sc in second ch from hook, * skip 2 ch, work 7 dc in next ch (shell made), skip 2 ch, sc in next ch *; repeat from * to * across chain, ending with 4 dc in last ch (half shell made).

2 Drop A; attach color B (yellow). With B, ch 1, turn. **Row 2**: With B, sc in first dc, ch 2, * work (yo and draw up loop in next stitch, yo and draw through 2 loops of dc, retaining last loop dc on hook) seven times (8 loops in all on hook).

3 Yo and draw through all loops on hook (cluster made), ch 2.

Sc in next A stitch *. Repeat from * to * across, ending ch 2; work dc in each of last 4 ch, retaining last loop of each (5 loops on hook). Yo and draw through all loops on hook (half cluster made).

5 Ch 3, turn. **Row 3**: With B, work 3 dc in joining st of half cluster below (half shell made), sc in next sc, * work 7 dc in joining stitch of next cluster, sc in next sc *. Repeat from * to * across.

Sunburst Pattern in Two Colors

6 With A, ch 3, turn. **Row 4**: Work half cluster on next 3 stitches, * ch 2, sc in next dc, ch 2, work cluster on next 7 stitches *; repeat from * to * across, ending ch 2, sc in last sc. Ch 1, turn. **Row 5**:

8 **Row 4**: Work half-cluster on 2 dc, * ch 2, sc in next dc, ch 2, work 5-dc cluster in next 5 stitches *; repeat from * to *, ending with ch 2, sc in top of ch-3. Change colors, ch 1, turn. **Row 5**: Sc in first sc, work 5-dc shell in next cluster, sc in next sc *; repeat from * to *. Change colors; ch 3, turn. Repeat Rows 2 through 5 for pattern.

Sc in first sc, * work shell in next cluster, sc in next sc *; repeat from * to * across, ending with 4-dc half shell in last half cluster. Repeat Rows 2 through 5 for pattern and alternate colors every 2 rows. Sample shows completed pattern.

7 A variation of this pattern uses only 5 dc for each shell and cluster and changes colors every row. Fasten off old color, attach new color at end of each row. Make chain with multiple of 6, plus 5. **Row 1**: Sc in second ch from hook, * skip 2 ch, work 5-dc in next ch, skip 2 ch, sc in next ch *; repeat from * across row, ending with 3 dc in last ch. Change colors; ch 1, turn. **Row 2**: Sc in first sc, * ch 2, work cluster on next 5 dc, ch 2, sc in next dc *; repeat from * to * across, ending with ch 2, work half cluster on last 3 stitches. Change colors; ch 3, turn. **Row 3**: Work 2-dc half shell in cluster, * sc in next sc, work 5-dc

9 Another variation uses just the shell stitch and 3 colors, changing colors each row. With color A, chain multiple of 6, plus 2. **Row 1**: Work as for Row 1 in Step 1, page 93, but ending with sc in last ch. Drop A; with B, ch 3, turn. **Row 2**: Work 2 dc in first sc (half shell), * sc in center dc of 5-dc shell, work 5 dc in next sc *; repeat from * to * across, working 3 dc in last sc. Drop B; with C, ch 1, turn. **Row 3**: Sc in first dc, * work 5-dc shell in next sc, sc in center dc of next shell *; repeat from * to * across, ending with sc in top of ch-3. Drop C; pick up A and ch 3, turn.

shell in next cluster *; repeat from * to * across, ending with sc in last sc. Change color; ch 3, turn.

10 Repeat Rows 2 and 3 for pattern, changing colors each row by picking previously dropped color and carrying strand (connecting rows) loosely along edge of work. Sample shows completed shell pattern.

Pattern Made with Loom

The basis of this pattern is a flower made on a loom available in craft stores (you can make your own with pegboard or wood and headless nails). Add a little embroidery and a little crocheting to make an attractive lace pattern.

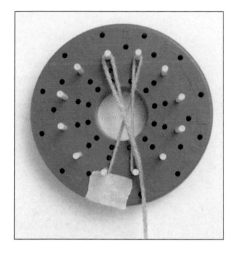

1 Arrange 12 evenly spaced pegs to form a circle with desired diameter. Tape end of yarn (we used yellow) to the loom next to a peg, * wrap yarn around corresponding peg on opposite side and bring it back around next peg to the right *; repeat from * to * wrapping yarn back and forth across loom and working counterclockwise.

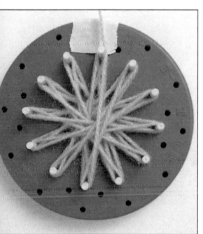

2 Continue to wrap yarn around pegs in this manner until each peg has 3 loops.

3 Cut yarn, leaving a long end. Thread end in a yarn needle and work a small circle of tiny backstitches around center to fasten loops securely in place. Fasten off yarn and trim away excess.

4 Gently lift flower off loom, one peg at a time.

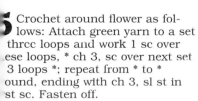

5 Crochet around flower as follows: Attach green yarn to a set three loops and work 1 sc over these loops, * ch 3, sc over next set 3 loops *; repeat from * to * around, ending with ch 3, sl st in first sc. Fasten off.

Pattern Made with Loom

8 You can also work a second green row so motifs can be joined as squares. **Row 2**: Ch 1, * sc in sc, work (3 dc over ch-3 arch, sc in next sc) twice, work (2 dc, ch 11) over next arch, sl st in eleventh ch from hook, dc over same arch (corner made) *; repeat from * to *. Sl st in first sc.

6 With a doubled strand of white yarn, embroider satin stitches, as shown, to cover the flower center (as defined by backstitches).

7 To join flowers as you work the green row, work (ch 3 and sc) around and, at places where edges of flowers touch, work sc in adjoining sc, then continue to work green row. Seven joined flowers form a hexagon.

10 Continue to join adjacent sides and corners as you add squares. Sample shows four square joined.

9 Make another motif (B), working Row 2 to third corner. At corner arch, work 2 dc over arch, ch 5, sl st in center of adjoining corner arch (on motif A), continuing on B, ch 5, sl st in first ch of corner chain just made, dc over same arch to complete corner, * sc in next sc, 2 dc over next arch, sl st in center dc of adjoining 3-dc group on A, dc over same arch on B *; repeat from * to * once more, sc in next sc, work corner, joining to motif A as before. Sl st to first sc.

Circular Patterns

Ch 7. Join with sl st to form ring. **Rnd 1**: Ch 4 (counts as first treble), work 19 more treble (tr) ring. Join to top of ch-4 with sl . **Rnd 2**: Ch 8 (counts as first double treble and ch 3), work double treble (dtr) in next tr.

2 Work (ch 3 and dtr) in each tr around, ending ch 3; join with sl st in fifth ch of ch-8. **Rnd 3**: Ch 4, dtr in next dtr.

3 Then * ch 6, work another dtr in same place as last one, retaining the last 2 loops on hook; work another dtr in next dtr, retaining last loop (3 loops on hook); yo and draw through all loops *.

Repeat from * to * around, ending with ch 6; join to top of ch- **Rnd 4**: Ch 1, work 4 sc over first -6 arch.

5 * Ch 5, sc in next ch-6 arch * ; repeat from * to * around, ending ch 5, treble in fourth ch of beginning arch, where 4 sc were worked. To make a larger piece, work as for last rnd, adding 1 chain more to each chain arch between sc as you work each successive rnd.

Circular Patterns

Another lace motif worked in rounds.

6 Ch 6 and join with sl st to form ring. **Rnd 1**: Ch 6 (counts as first dc and ch-3), work (dc, ch 3) in ring eleven times. Join with sl st to third ch of ch-6. **Rnd 2**: * Work (ch 3, sc in 3rd ch from hook) three times to make 3 picots.

7 Turn down last picot made and attach it with sc worked between first 2 picots.

8 Ch 3, sc in third ch from hook (another picot made); work sc before first picot (a picot spoke made).

9 Work 2 sc in next ch-3 arch in circle *; repeat from * to * around. Join with sl st to first stitch. Fasten off. Attach yarn to third picot (at outer edge) of first 4-picot group.

10 **Rnd 3**: Sc where yarn was attached, work (ch 3, work 2 sc at top of next picot spoke) eleven times, ch 3, sl st in first sc. **Rnd 4**: Sl st in first ch of ch-3 arch, sc over same arch, work (ch 8, sc over next arch) eleven times around, ending with ch 4, work treble in first sc. To make a larger piece, work as for last rnd, adding 1 chain to each arch between sc on each successive rnd.

Three-Dimensional Stitches

These stitches are fairly easy to work, yet give rich texture to your crocheting.

Worked in single crochet

1 Work 2 rows of sc. **Row 3**: * Sc in 3 sc, draw up a loop in next sc and ch 4; yo and draw through both loops on hook (textured stitch made) *.

2 Repeat from * to * across, ending with sc stitches. **Row 4 and all even-numbered rows**: Sc in each sc across. **Row 5**: Sc in first 5 sc, work textured stitch as before, * sc in next 3 sc, work textured stitch *; repeat from * to * across, ending with sc. **Row 6**: Work as for Row 4. Repeat rows 3 through 6 for pattern. Sample shows completed pattern.

Worked in double crochet

3 Work 2 rows of dc. **Row 3**: * Work dc in 3 dc, yo, and insert hook from right to left under the post of next dc.

4 Yo and draw up a loop, (yo and draw up another loop in same place) twice more (7 loops on hook); yo and draw through all loops on hook (cluster st worked around post). * Repeat from * to * across. Work Row 4 and all even-number rows in dc.

5 On next row, work 5 dc before first cluster to alternate placement of clusters. Repeat from Row 3 for pattern.

Three-Dimensional Stitches

Popcorns

6 Work 2 rows of dc. **Row 3**: Dc in first 4 dc, work 4 dc in next dc, remove hook from loop, and insert in the first of the 4 dc just made, then pick up dropped loop.

Horizontal pineapple

8 Work 2 rows of dc. Work 3 (or 5) dc; work pineapple as follows: dc, retaining last loop (2 loops on hook).

7 Draw this loop through the firs dc, ch 1 to secure stitch (popcorn made). Work popcorns in this manner, spacing them throughout work or working them in groups to form geometric patterns as shown above. Work a dc between popcorns when working them in groups.

9 * Yo, insert hook right to left under post of last 2 dc (unfinished dc and previous one), and draw up loop *; repeat from * to * once more (6 loops on hook).

10 Yo and draw through all loop on hook (pineapple made), then work (dc in next 4 dc, work pineapple) across row. Work a row o dc, followed by pineapple row, alternating spacing between those on pre vious pineapple row. Sample shows completed horizontal pineapple patte

Geometric Shapes in Two Colors

3 **Rnd 2**: Attach color B (blue) to first ch of any arch between clusters. Ch 3 (first dc) and work 3 more dc over same arch, work 4 dc in next arch, * ch 6, work 4 dc over each of next 2 arches *; repeat from * to * once more, ch 6. Join with sl st to top of ch-3.

Triangles can be joined to form a larger triangle, or joined in strips (alternating wide base and points along one edge), then strips can be joined for an afghan.

Triangle

1 With color A (yellow, as shown), ch 4. Join with sl st to form ring. **Rnd 1**: Ch 4, * yo twice and draw up a loop in ring, work (yo and draw through 2 loops) twice * (2 loops remain on hook); repeat from * to * three more times (5 loops on hook); yo and draw through all loops on hook (a cluster made).

Granny square

4 With color A (yellow), ch 6. Join with sl st to form ring. **Rnd 1**: Ch 3 (first dc), work 2 dc in ring, work (ch 3, 3 dc in ring) three times, ch 3. Join with sl st to top of initial ch-3. Fasten off.

2 Work (ch 4 and 4-tr cluster) five more times in ring, ch 4, join with sl st to fourth ch of initial ch-4. Fasten off.

5 Attach color B (purple) to any ch-3 corner. **Rnd 2**: Ch 3, 2 dc over ch-3, ch 3, work 3 more dc over ch-3 (first corner made), * ch 3, work (3 dc, ch 3, 3 dc) at next corner *; repeat from * to * twice more, ch 3. Join to top of ch-3. Fasten off. **Rnd 3**: Attach A to any corner. Work first corner as before, * ch 3, work 3 dc over next ch-3, ch 3, work (3 dc, ch 3, 3 dc) over corner ch-3 *; repeat from * to * twice more, ch 3, work 3 dc over next ch-3, ch 3. Join to top of ch-3. Fasten off. **Rnd 4**: Attach B to any corner and work first corner as before, then * work (ch 3, 3 dc over next ch-3) twice along side, ch 3, work (3 dc, ch 3, 3 dc) over corner ch-3 *; repeat from * to * twice, then work (ch 3, 3 dc over ch-3) twice, ch 3. Join to top of ch-3. Fasten off. For a larger square, continue to alternate colors and work corners and sides as on last rnd, adding another (ch 3, 3 dc over ch-3) along each side on each successive rnd. Granny squares are a traditional crocheted square and are a popular way to use up scraps of leftover yarn.

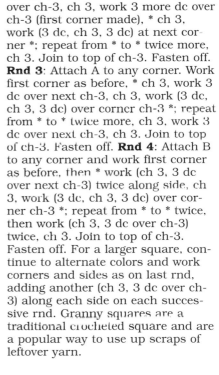

Geometric Shapes in Two Colors

7 **Rnd 3**: Attach color B (yellow) to any ch-7 arch. Ch 2 (first hdc), work (2 dc, 3 tr, 2 dc, hdc) over same ch-7 arch, work (hdc, 2 dc, 3 tr, 2 dc, hdc) over next 5 ch-7 arches. Join with sl st to top of ch-2. Fasten off.

Hexagons made this way can be used as trim by sewing them neatly in place onto the other piece. They are also good for making borders.

9 **Rnd 2**: Attach color B (dark blue) to any ch-2 corner and ch 5 (first double treble). Work (2 dtr, ch 2, 3 dtr) over same corner, then work (3 dtr, ch 2, 3 dtr) over each remaining ch-2 corner. Join to top of ch-5. Fasten off.

Flower hexagon

6 With color A (green), ch 6. Join with sl st to form ring. **Rnd 1**: Ch 4 (first treble), work 2 more treble (tr) in ring, ch 1, work (3 tr in ring, ch 1) five more times. Join with sl st to top of ch-4. **Rnd 2**: Ch 1, sc in top of ch-4, then work (ch 7, sc in next ch-1) six more times. Sl st in first sc to join. Fasten off.

Tile hexagon

8 With color A (light blue), ch 6. Join with sl st to form ring. **Rnd 1**: Ch 3, 2 dc in ring, work (ch 2, 3 dc) in ring five times, ch 2. Join with sl st to top of ch-3. Fasten off.

10 **Rnd 3**: Attach A to sl st at joining and ch 1*. Sc in each dtr to next corner ch-2, work (2 sc, ch 1, 2 sc) over corner ch-2; repeat from * around, working sc in last 3 dtr. Join to first stitch at beginning. Fasten off. These hexagons can be joined along the edges to form an afghan or table covering.

Embroidering Over Crochet

Cross stitch

Cross stitches are usually worked over single crochet stitches, since these crocheted stitches are fairly square (as many stitches across as rows worked per inch). The result are well-formed cross stitches. The stitches are worked sewing through the small openings at the "corners" of each stitch. If desired, follow a charted cross-stitch design.

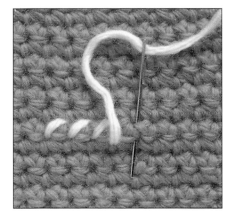

1 Use a tapestry needle for embroidering. Anchor yarn on wrong side of work, then bring needle forward through small opening between stitches at lower left of stitch to be covered and reinsert it at upper right opening. For stitches in a row, work first half of all cross stitches in row as shown.

2 Embroider other half of cross stitches working back across stitches and using same openings for needle as before. Work single cross stitches the same way using four openings at corners of each stitch. In any design, be sure top strand of each stitch crosses in same direction.

Backstitch

Worked with a double stand of yarn, this stitch is ideal for double crochet pieces.

3 Bring needle forward between 2 dc. * Reinsert needle under dc on right and bring it forward again after one stitch on left *.

4 Repeat from * to * to work several backstitches in a row. If you wish to skip a stitch, bring needle out again 2 stitches to left of where yarn last emerged.

5 Sample shows rows of backstitches worked in groups and singly in alternating colors.

Embroidering Over Crochet

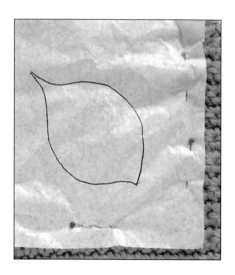

Stem stitch

Work on any base of compactly worked crochet stitches, such as sc or hdc.

6 Before embroidering, mark outlines of design on crochet piece by basting with white thread. Work simple shapes freehand. For more intricate shapes, trace design onto tissue paper and pin tracing to crochet. Baste along traced lines, then gently tear away tissue paper, leaving sewn stitches in place.

8 Sample shows a piece of crochet embroidered in stem stitch.

7 Anchor yarn on back of crochet and pull tapestry needle (threaded with yarn) forward at start of design. Following basted line, embroider stem stitch, reinserting needle a short distance beyond where it emerged. Bring it out again about halfway back to start of first stitch and repeat process.

Chain stitch

Use on a background of compactly crocheted stitches.

9 Mark outlines for design as described in step 6 above. Bring needle to front at starting point, make a small loop of yarn and, holding loop in place with left thumb, reinsert needle back at starting point; let it come out again a small distance ahead to catch loop under needle as shown. Make another loop, hold it in place, and stitch in and out as before, catching new loop.

10 Work chain stitch along outline, then work more chain stitch inside outline to fill in whole area as shown.

Loops and Buttons

When you add an edging to a garment, you can make one like this (shown here in green) with loops in the design that can also function as buttonholes.

1 **Row 1**: Work a row of sc along edge, working about 1 sc for each row of sc, or spacing stitches as needed to keep edge flat.

2 Fasten off at end of row. **Row 2**: Attach yarn to beginning of first row, ch 1, sc in first and each remaining sc across. Fasten off.

3 **Row 3**: Attach yarn to beginning of last row. Ch 1, work (sc in 3 sc, ch 3, skip 1 sc) across section to be used for buttonholes, then work remaining section in sc as before, or continue to work loop pattern as a decorative edge even where buttonholes are not needed.

4 **Row 4**: Do not fasten off, but work a row of reverse sc (see page 37), working left to right in each sc and in each ch of loops.

5 Complete row and fasten off. Sample shows completed edging.

Loops and Buttons

For a custom look, you can also make small or large buttons with yarn, a crochet hook, a plastic ring, and some cotton.

Flat button

6 Use a plastic ring of desired size (available at craft stores). Attach yarn to ring. Inserting hook into center of ring as if working on a crocheted chain ring; work sc around, covering ring. Join with sl st to first sc. Fasten off.

Ball button

8 Ch 3. In third ch from hook, work 6 dc. Do not join but work around in a spiral. **Rnd 2**: Work 2 sc in each sc (12 sc). **Rnd 3**: Sc in each sc around. Piece will be cupped to form a half sphere.

7 Turn tops of stitches just made to center of ring. With yarn (of same or contrasting color) threaded in yarn needle, sew the stitch tops together at center of ring, crossing threads in a decorative way as shown.

9 **Rnd 4**: * Draw up a loop in each of next 2 sc, yo, and draw through all 3 loops on hook (dec made) *; repeat from * to * around (6 sc). Stuff button firmly with a bit of cotton or scraps of matching yarn.

10 **Rnd 5**: Work sc dec as before around (3 sc). Fasten off, leaving an end. Thread end into yarn needle and draw last 3 stitches tightly together; sew button in place, anchoring yarn on wrong side of work.

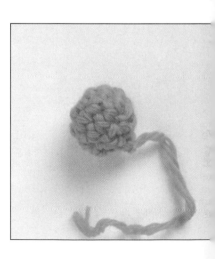

Working with Beads

Beads can be used to embellish crocheted garments. They also add a nice finishing touch to a lace pattern or the edge of a curtain. They can even be used on pillows!

1 First figure out how many beads to use. Decide where to place beads in work, how many to use per row, and how many rows you expect to make from a ball of yarn. The thickness of yarn determines the beads to use since the holes must accommodate the yarn. For example, small glass beads can be used on fine threads and large wooden beads on thicker yarn. Then thread the determined number of beads onto yarn.

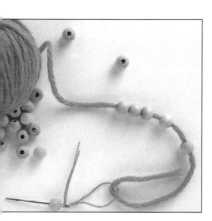

2 A good way is to thread a double strand of sewing thread through a needle, loop end first as shown. Draw yarn end through thread loop. Then thread the beads onto the needle, passing them carefully over the thread loop onto the crochet yarn.

3 When all the beads are threaded onto the yarn, slide them down the yarn toward the ball to keep a small part of the yarn free and yet keep the beads within reach. Wrap excess the yarn, with beads distributed along it, around the ball.

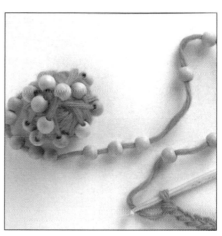

5 Sample shows beaded single crochet where every other sc is beaded and the position of the beads is alternated on beaded rows.

Working beads in single crochet

4 Position beads in work only as you work a wrong-side row. Work to where you wish to insert a bead, then work sc as follows: yo and draw up loop, slide bead up to work; yo and draw through both loops to completed beaded sc. Repeat process each time you wish to insert a bead in work.

Working with Beads

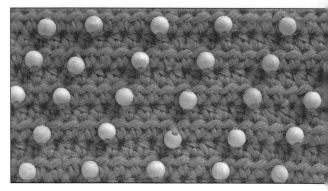

Working beads in half double crochet

6 Work beading on wrong-side rows. To work beaded hdc, yo and draw up loop, slide bead up to work; yo and draw through all 3 loops to complete beaded hdc.

7 Sample shows beaded half double crochet with 3 plain hdc worked between beaded hdc across row and where the position on the beaded hdc was shifted 1 hdc to the left (on wrong side row) of beaded hdc below, forming diagonal lines of beads on right side.

9 Insert a bead on *right side* as follows: Ch 5, insert hook under next arch, and draw up a loop; slide bead up to front of this loop, then reaching behind work, catch yarn with hook and draw it through both loops on hook to complete beaded sc.

Working bead on diamond net stitch

8 See page 33 for pattern. Work the insertion of beads on every row (after the first) for this pattern. Insert a bead on *wrong side* as follows: Ch, insert hook under next arch, and draw up a loop; slide bead up to work; yo and draw through both loops on hook to complete beaded sc over arch. Repeat process for each sc across row.

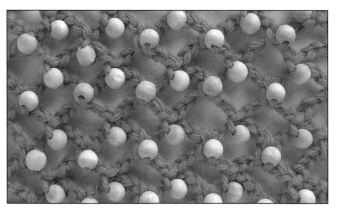

10 Sample shows beaded diamond net stitch. Worked in raffia or corded yarn, this pattern could make an attractive tote bag.

Borders

These little borders can embellish
dishtowels or add elegance to linen
napkins, using a thin yarn.

Simple and fast-to-make border

1 Make a chain with multiple of 16, plus 5. **Row 1**: Sc in second ch from hook and in each remaining ch across. Ch 6, turn. **Row 2**: Skip first 3 sc (turning ch counts as first dc and ch-3), dc in next dc *, ch 3, skip next 3 sc, dc in next sc *; repeat from * to * across. Ch 1, turn. **Row 3**: Sc in first dc, work 3 sc over next ch-3 arch, * ch 6, skip next arch, work double treble (dtr) in next dc, retaining last loop on hook, work 2 dtr over next arch, retaining last loop of each hook (4 loops on hook); yo and draw through all loops.

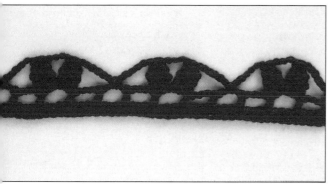

Ch 4, work 2 more dtr over same arch, retaining last loop of each; work dtr in next dc, retaining last loop (4 loops on hook); yo and draw through all loops, then ch 6, skip next arch and dc, sc over next arch *; repeat from * to *, ending row with 3 sc over last arch, sc in third ch of ch-6. Fasten off. Sample shows completed border.

Yo four times and, inserting hook below ch-6 arch, draw up a loop; work (yo and draw through first 2 loops on hook) twice (4 loops on hook); yo twice and draw up a loop over next ch-6 arch (7 loops on hook).

Clover border

3 Make chain with multiple of 11, plus 2. **Row 1**: Sc in second ch from hook and in each remaining ch across. Ch 1, turn. **Row 2**: Sc in first sc, * ch 6, then 3 ch, sl st in third ch from hook (picot made), ch 6, skip 6 sc, sc in next sc *; repeat from * to * across. Ch 7, turn. **Row 3**: * Work (3 double treble in the picot, retaining last loop of each; yo and draw through all 4 loops on hook, ch 5) twice, then work 3 double treble (dtr) in same picot, retaining last loop of each; yo and draw through all loops.

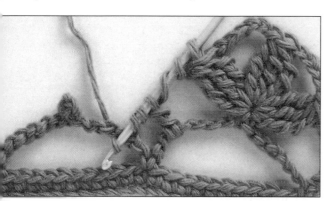

5 Yo and draw through 2 loops at a time until only 1 remains *; repeat from * to *across, ending with last 3-dtr group, then ch 7, sl st in last sc. Fasten off. Sample showns completed clover border.

Borders

Picot border

6 Make a chain with multiple of 8, plus 4. **Row 1**: Dc in sixth ch from hook, * ch 1, skip 1 ch, dc in next ch *; repeat across chain. Ch 6, turn. **Row 2**: Dc in first dc, * ch 5, skip next 3 dc, work (dc, ch 5, dc) in next dc *; repeat from * to * across, ending with ch 5; skip 3 dc, skip next ch after skipped dc, in next ch work (dc, ch 3, dc). Ch 5, turn. **Row 3**: Dc over ch-3 arch, ch 2, * work sc over next ch-5 arch, then work (ch 2 and dc) three times over next arch, ch 2 *.

Arched border

8 Make chain with multiple of 26, plus 3. **Row 1**: Sc in second ch from hook and in each remaining ch. Ch 6, turn. **Row 2**: Dc in first sc, * ch 2, skip 4 sc, work (dc in next sc, ch 1, skip 1 sc) twice, dc in next dc, ch 8, skip 8 sc, work (dc in next sc, ch 1, skip 1 sc) twice, dc in next sc (3-dc unit made), ch 2, skip 4 sc, work (dc, ch 7, dc) in next sc *; repeat from * to *, ending last repeat with (dc, ch 3, dc) in last sc. Ch 4, turn. **Row 3**: Work 5 treble (tr) over ch-3 arch, * ch 2, sc in center dc of 3-dc unit, ch 6, sc over ch-8, ch 6, sc in center dc of next 3-dc unit, ch 2, work 11 tr over next ch-7 arch (photograph at left).* Repeat from * to * across, ending with 6 tr over last arch (formed by turning chain). Ch 4, turn. **Row 4**: Tr in first tr, ch 6, tr again in same place as last tr, retaining last loop on hook; then tr in next 2 tr, retaining last loop of each; then yo and draw through all 4 loops on hook (3-tr cluster made), ch 6 (photograph below).

7 Repeat from * to * across, ending with sc over last ch-5 arch, ch 2, work (dc, ch 2, dc) over turning ch. Ch 1, turn. **Row 4**: Work ch 3 more, sl st in third ch from hook (picot made), * work (2 sc over next ch-2) four times, make a picot as before *; repeat from * to * across, ending with last 2 sc over turning ch, make picot. Fasten off. Sample shows completed picot border.

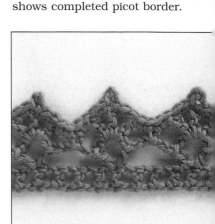

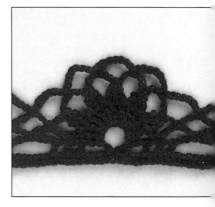

10 **Row 5**: Sc in first arch, wor (ch 4, sc in next arch), across, ending with treble treble (tr tr) in last stitch. Fasten off. Sample shows completed arch border.

9 Work 3-tr cluster as before, * ch 2, sc over ch-6 arch, ch 6, sc over next arch, ch 2, 3-tr cluster in first 3 tr of 11-tr group, work (ch 6, 3-tr cluster) four more times, always working first tr where last tr of previous cluster was made, as you work around 11-tr group *; repeat from * to * across, ending with (3-tr cluster, ch 6) twice in last 5 tr; ch 6, 2-tr cluster in top of ch-4. Ch 9, turn.

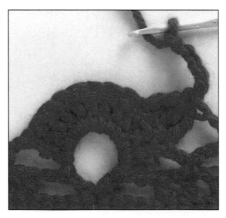

Trims Made with Crocheted Ribbon

Various types of ribbon you crochet yourself can be turned into attractive trims for garments or household items. Sketch the planned design in its actual size onto paper so you can pin the ribbon in place to finish trim.

Making the ribbon

1 Ch 2 and work sc in second loop from hook.

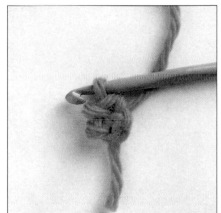

2 Turn work and insert the hook into loop of first ch and then into the beginning loop of stitch (3 loops on hook). (Yo and draw through 2 loops) twice.

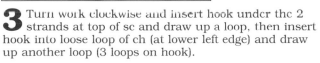

3 Turn work clockwise and insert hook under the 2 strands at top of sc and draw up a loop, then insert hook into loose loop of ch (at lower left edge) and draw up another loop (3 loops on hook).

4 (Yo and draw through 2 loops) twice.

5 Turn work clockwise. Draw up a loop in sc just made and in loose loop just below (along left edge). Repeat steps 4 and 5 for length desired. Check length to the design sketch; add or eliminate rows to adjust length if needed.

Trims Made with Crocheted Ribbon

6 Work a row of sl st along one side edge of ribbon, working a stitch for each loop on the ribbon.

7 Pin the ribbon to the design outline.

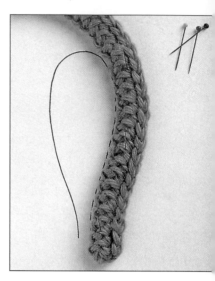

8 Thread the finishing yarn (we used contrasting color for visibility) into yarn needle and anchor yarn under threads of ribbon as shown. Bring needle out about 10 loops below center top of curve as shown. Insert the needle from bottom up through corresponding loop on opposite side of curve. Then move needle under the joining strand of yarn and insert it from bottom up through loop at center top of curve.

10 Work 6 blanket stitches (see page 60) over the side yarn loop, working to center; then thread yarn up through top loop and work 8 blanket stitches back to center. Work 6 blanket stitches to end at left side. Fasten off, concealing yarn end in ribbon stitches.

9 Pass the needle through the loop created at the right side and bring it from bottom up through the beginning loop of the left side. Then bring the needle up through the loop at top and insert it from bottom up back in loop at right edge (loops now joined at center of design).

Ribbon Border

This crocheted ribbon forms a border that can be worked separately
and sewn in place, or joined to piece
as you crochet. It can even be fash-
ioned to use as a centerpiece.

Work 4 more sc on chain. Insert
hook into next ch and then into
urteenth sc from hook; yo and
ork sc.

Basic pattern

1 Work with 2 separate balls of
yarn. Use 1 ball to crochet a
length of foundation chain, and,
without fastening off, secure last
loop with a safety pin to keep chains
from unraveling. With the other ball
of yarn, start with the first ch of the
foundation chain and sc in 14 ch.

2 Insert the hook in the next
chain and then into the first sc
to form a ring; yo and work sc (first
joining made).

3 Work 16 more sc on chain,
insert hook into fourth sc after
the first joining and work sc to join.
Always check that you have the
proper section of ribbon for the top
layer at each joining.

5 Repeat steps 2 through 4 for desired length, adding
more chains to the foundation chain, as needed,
with the first ball of yarn. Fasten off. Neatly sew the
border to fabric edge.

Ribbon Border

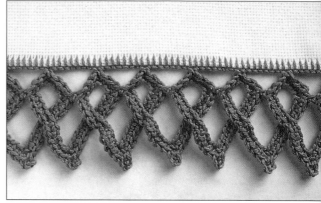

Border worked directly onto fabric

6 Embroider a row of blanket stitches along fabric edge. Make a foundation chain. With separate ball of yarn, crochet sc in first 7 chains of foundation. Inserting hook from bottom up through corresponding blanket stitch (seventh stitch from left edge of fabric), work sl st to join to fabric, then sc in next 7 ch. To make first loop of ribbon, insert hook in next chain, then into first sc of ribbon and draw up a loop; yo and complete sc (ribbon joining made), * sc in next 6 ch, then ch 3, sc in third ch from hook (picot made), sc in next 13 ch.

7 Skip 7 blanket stitches along fabric edge and join ribbon to fabric as before in next blanket stitch. Sc in next 3 ch, insert hook through next ch and then into fourth sc on previous loop (counting from first loop joining), work sc to join. Work sc on next 4 ch, insert hook in next ch, then in the seventh sc after picot to draw up loop; yo and complete sc (another loop joining made) *; repeat from * to * across. Fasten off.

9 Chain 201. Work sc in second ch from hook, sc in next 5 ch, then inserting hook from bottom up, sl st in any sc of crocheted center to join. Sc in next 6 ch, insert hook in next ch and in first sc of ribbon and draw up loop, yo and complete sc (ribbon loop made).

Centerpiece

8 Ch 12 and join with sl st to form a ring. **Rnd 1**: Ch 1, work 16 sc in ring. Join with sl st to first sc. **Rnd 2**: Ch 5 (first dc and ch 2), dc in next sc, work (dc, ch 2) in each remaining sc around. Join with sl st in third ch of ch-5. **Rnd 3**: Ch 1, sc in same ch as joining, * work 2 sc over next ch-2, sc in next dc *; repeat from * to *, ending with 2 sc over last ch-2. Join. **Rnd 4**: Ch 1, sc in each sc around. Fasten off. A fabric disk bordered with blanket stitch can be substituted for this crocheted center.

10 * Sc in next 18 ch, skip 5 sc along circle edge, insert hook from bottom through next sc on circle and sl st to join work. Sc in next 6 ch, insert hook in next ch and in thirteenth sc from last loop joining, draw up loop; yo and complete this loop joining *; repeat from * to * six more times, then sc in last 12 ch. Join with sl st to first sc of ribbon at base of first loop. Fasten off.

Background Patterns for Irish Lace

hese patterns are often used to onnect the large motifs in Irish ce, but they can also be used by hemselves to create beautiful curins.

iamonds with picots

1 Make a chain with a multiple of 7, plus 2. **Row 1**: Sc in second h from hook, * ch 2, then ch 5 ore, sl st in fifth ch from hook picot made), ch 3, make picot as efore, ch 2, skip 6 ch, sc in next ch repeat from * to * across. Ch 6, rn. **Row 2**: Work picot, ch 2, sc ver center of next arch (between icots), * ch 2, picot, ch 3, picot, ch , sc over center of next arch *. epeat from * to * across ending ch , picot, ch 2, tr in last sc. Ch 1, rn.

iamonds with shamrocks

3 Make chain with multiple of 10, plus 2. **Row 1**: Sc in second ch om hook, * ch 6, work shamrock s follow: work (ch 7, sl st in sev- nth ch from hook) three times, sl st ch that precedes the first loop of hamrock (shamrock made).

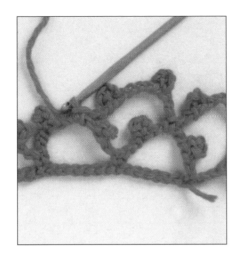

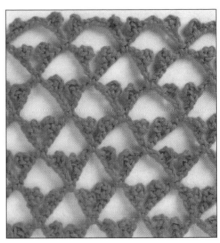

2 **Row 3**: Sc over next ch, *ch 2, picot, ch 3, picot, ch 2, sc over next arch *; repeat from * to *, end- ing skip 1 ch after last picot, sc in next ch. Ch 6, turn. Repeat Rows 2 and 3 for desired length. Fasten off.

5 **Row 3**: * Ch 6 more, work shamrock, ch 6, sc between first 2 petal on next shamrock below, ch 1 (in back of center petal for right side row) and sc between last 2 petals of shamrock *; repeat from * to * across. Ch 7, turn.

Repeat Rows 2 and 3 for pattern, working to desired length. Fasten off.

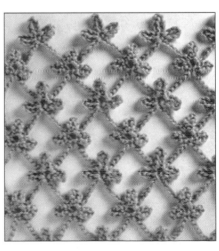

4 Ch 6, skip 9 ch, sc in next ch *; repeat from * to * across. Ch 7, turn. **Row 2**: * Ch 6 more, work shamrock, ch 6, sc between first 2 petals of next shamrock below, ch 1 (in front of center petal for wrong side row) and sc between last 2 petals of shamrock *; repeat from * to * across. Ch 7, turn.

Background Patterns for Irish Lace

Diamonds with bobbles

6 Make chain with multiple of 8, plus 2. **Row 1**: Sc in second ch from hook, * ch 4, work bobble as follows: ch 4, turn work, work (draw up a loop in next ch, reach under chain to draw up another loop) four times (9 loops on hook).

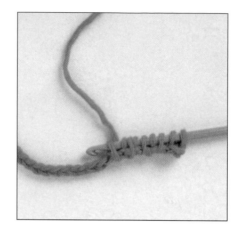

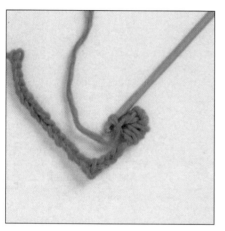

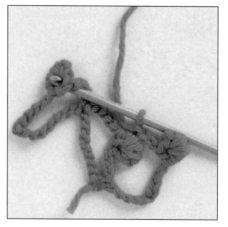

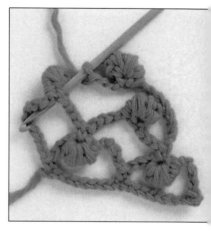

7 Yo and draw through all loops on hook; ch 1 to fasten (bobble made).

8 Ch 4, skip 7 ch of foundation chain, sc in next ch *; repeat from * to * across. Ch 5, turn. **Row 2**: * Ch 4 more, make bobble as before, ch 4, then inserting hook *from back to front* under ch-1, fastening stitch on next bobble, work sc *.

9 Repeat from * to * across. Ch 5 turn. **Row 3**: * Ch 4 more, mak bobble as before, ch 4, then inserting hook *from front* under ch-1 of next bobble, work sc.

10 Repeat from * to * across. Repeat Rows 2 and 3 for pattern working to desired length. Fasten off.

Lacy Square

The first square is made completely as a single unit. From the second square on, join each new square as you crochet the last row. Join squares in long rows to use as borders for sheets and towels. Joining to make a corner produces a border for a tablecloth or mat.

Joining squares to form a large rectangular piece can produce beautiful curtains or even a whole tablecloth. The choice is yours!

1 Ch 8 and join to the first ch with a sl st to form a ring. **Row 1:** Ch 4 (counts as first dtr), work 3 double treble (dtr) in ring, retaining the last loop of each on hook; yo and draw through all 4 loops at once (first cluster made).

2 * Ch 9, dtr in ring, ch 9, work 4 dtr in ring, retaining last loop of each; yo and draw through all 5 loops to complete cluster *; repeat from * to * twice more, ending ch 9, dtr in ring, ch 5, work treble (tr) in top of first cluster.

3 **Row 2:** * Ch 5, sc over next ch-9 arch, ch 5, work (tr, ch 5, tr) in next dtr (corner made), ch 5, sc over next arch *; repeat from * to * three more times, ending with sl st (not sc) in tr of last arch. Fasten off. The first square is completed.

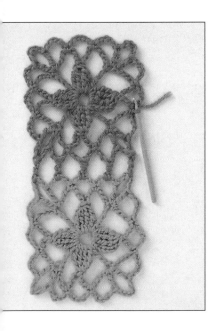

4 For second square (shown in orange), work as for first square until Row 1 is completed. **Row 2:** * Ch 5, sc over next arch, ch 5, work (tr, ch 5, tr) in next dtr for corner, ch 5, sc in next arch *; repeat from * to * once more, then ch 5, sc in next arch, ch 5, now begin joining at corner as follows: tr in next dtr, ch 3, then work dc over corner ch-5 of previous (blue) square (be sure the front of each square faces up), ch 2, work another tr in same dtr of corner on new (orange) square, work (ch 3, dc over next arch on previous square, ch 2, sc in next arch on new square) three times, ending last repeat with tr worked in next dtr; then ch 3, dc over ch-5 of corner on previous square, ch 2, tr in same dtr on new square to complete corner and joining, then ch 5, sl st in top of tr (at first cluster). Fasten off.

5 Make third square (orange) in same manner as second, joining it below one of the joined pair to form a corner as shown. Join squares in an open rectangle to form a border for tablecloths or mats.

Lacy Square

6 The new square (orange) completes the unit and is joined along two sides. Make new square same as for first (see previous page) until Row 1 is done. **Row 2**: Ch 5, sc over next ch-9 arch, ch 5, work (tr, ch 5, tr) in next dtr for corner, ch 5, work (sc over next arch, ch 5) twice, join as follows: tr in next dtr, ch 3, work dc over corner ch-5 of old (blue) square, dc in over corner of square adjacent to next side (shown above new square), ch 2, work another tr in same dtr on new square, work (ch 3, dc over next arch on old square, ch 2, sc on next arch of new square) three times, ending last repeat with tr worked in next dtr; then ch 3, dc over corner ch-5 on old square.

7 Now work along top edge joining the adjacent old square as follows: work dc in old square (in photograph on right), ch 2.

8 Work another tr in same dtr on new square (photograph at center left).

9 Work (ch 3, dc over next arch on old square, ch 2, sc on next arch of new square: photograph at center right) three times, ending last repeat with tr in next dtr.

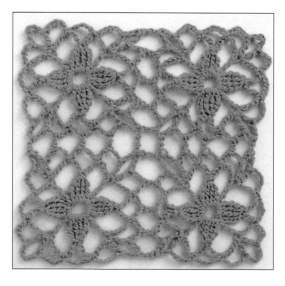

10 Then ch 3, dc over corner ch-5 on old square, ch 2, tr in same dtr to complete corner and joining, then ch 5, sl st in top of tr above first cluster. Sample shows completed unit with four squares.

Dainty Edgings

These pretty little edgings can add elegance to tablecloths, napkins, linen handkerchiefs, or even trim garments. Use a fine thread suitable for the fabric being trimmed. You can work the edging on a chain (as directions below indicate) or attach it directly to fabric that is finished with a row of blanket stitch (see page 60).

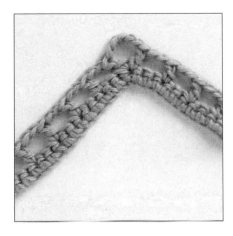

1 Make a chain with a multiple of 3, plus 2. **Row 1**: Sc in second ch from hook and in each remaining ch across. Ch 3, turn. **Row 2**: * Work (ch 2, skip 2 sc, dc in sc) until you reach spot for corner, then work ch 5, dc in same sc as last dc *; repeat from * to *. Ch 1, turn.

2 **Row 3**: Sc in top of dc, work (sc, then ch 3 and sl st in third ch from hook for picot, sc) over next ch-2 arch, * work (sc in next dc, 2 sc over next ch-2) three times, sc in next dc, sc over next ch-2, ch 5, turn to work over stitches just made, skip 3 sc, work (dc, ch 5, dc) in next sc, ch 5, skip 3 sc, sc in next sc.

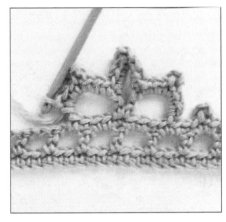

3 Ch 1, turn. Work (3 sc, picot, 3 sc) over each of the 3 ch-5 arches just made, then sc in same ch-2 where last sc was worked before turning, sc in next dc *; repeat from * to * until 2 ch-2 arches remain before next corner. (You may need to adjust placement of arched motifs, working more or fewer stitches between them.)

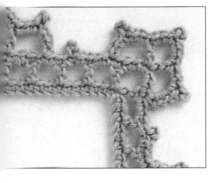

4 For corner, work (sc, picot, sc) over next arch, sc in dc, 2 sc over next arch, sc in dc, 5 sc over ch-5 arch, sc in dc. Ch 5, turn. Work (dc, ch 5, dc) in third sc of 5-sc, ch 5, skip 2 sc, sc in next sc. Ch 1, turn. Work (3 sc, picot, 3 sc) over each ch-5 arch, then work 2 sc over next ch-2 and continue along edge as before.

An easier variation

5 Work on a chain with a multiple of 12, plus 2. Work Rows 1 and 2 as above. **Row 3**: Sc in top of ch-3, * work 2 sc over next ch-2 arch, work sc and picot in next dc, work (2 sc over next arch, sc in dc) three times. Ch 9, turn. Skip next 5 sc, sc in next sc. Ch 1, turn. Work (3 sc, picot) three times over ch-9 arch *; repeat from * to *, adjusting placement as needed, to complete an arch just before corner, work (sc in 2 sc, picot, skip 1 sc, sc in 2 sc) in corner ch; then work (sc in dc, 2 sc over ch-2) twice, sc in dc. Ch 9, turn to work motif. Continue to work as before along edge.

Dainty Edgings

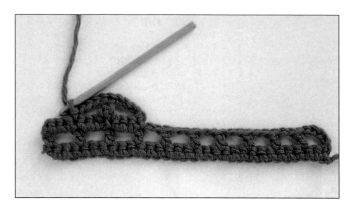

A more complex version

6 This pattern starts in a chain with a multiple of 21, plus 2. Work the first 2 rows as on previous page.
Row 3: Sc in top of dc-3, * 2 sc over next ch-2, sc in dc, 2 sc over ch-2, picot, sc in dc, 2 sc over ch-2, sc in dc. Ch 9, turn. Skip 7 sc, sc in next sc. Ch 1, turn.

7 Work (3 sc, picot, 7 sc, picot, 3 sc) over ch-9 arch, then work (2 sc over ch-2 arch, sc in dc) twice, 2 sc over next arch, picot, sc in dc, 2 sc over next arch, sc in dc. Ch 9, turn. Skip 7 sc, sc in next sc. Ch, turn. Work (3 sc, picot, 3 sc) over ch-9 arch.

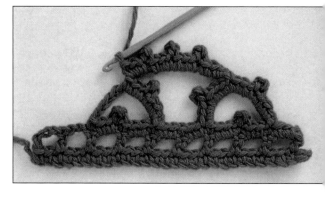

8 Ch 9, turn. Sc in center sc of the 7-sc group made on the previous arch.

9 Ch 1, turn. Over ch-9 arch just made work (3 sc, picot) three more times, then 3 more sc.

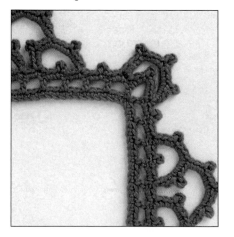

10 Work (3 sc, picot, 3 sc) on second half of unfinished arch, work 2 sc over next ch-arch, picot, sc in dc *; repeat from * to * to next corner. At corner, work (3 sc, picot, 2 sc) over ch-5 chain, then sc in dc. Ch 9, turn. Sl st to last sc made on the other side of corner, making a second arch over the corner. Ch 1, turn. Work (3 sc, picot) three times over ch-9 arch, then add 3 more sc, work 2 sc in ch-2 arch. Continue working edging in this manner.

Crocheted Trimming

Colorful strips of crochet, worked lengthwise, can enliven purchased garments or household items. The thickness and texture of the yarn, and the colors chosen for it, can make trimmings worked in the same directions produce quite different looks.

In three colors

1 With color A (pea green), make a chain with a multiple of 6, plus 2. **Row 1**: Sc in second ch from hook and in each remaining ch. Ch 3, turn. **Row 2**: Work 2 dc in first sc (3 dc, counting ch-3), skip 2 sc, sc in next sc, * skip 2 sc, work 5 dc in next sc (shell made).

2 Skip 2 sc, sc in next sc *. Repeat from * to *, ending with 3 dc in last sc (half shell). Fasten off. **Row 3**: Attach color B (yellow) with sl st at top of ch-3 at beginning of Row 2. Ch 1, sc in sl st just made, * ch 2, work (dc in next stitch, retaining last loop on hook) five times; yo and draw through all 6 loops on hook (cluster worked on 5 stitches), ch 2, sc in dc (at center of shell) *; repeat from * to * across, ending with sc in last dc of half shell. Fasten off.

3 **Row 4**: Attach color C (bright pink) to first sc. Ch 1, sc in sl st just made, * work 2 sc over next ch-2 arch, work ch 3, sc in second ch from hook, hdc in next ch (picot made), work 2 sc over next ch-2 arch *; repeat from * to * across, ending with sc in last sc. Fasten off.

4 Turn work to work other half. Attach color A to unworked loop of first ch on foundation chain. Working across foundation chain, work as for Row 2. Fasten off.

5 Work Row 3, then Row 4 just as on first side of trim. Sample shows completed tricolored trimming.

Crocheted Trimming

In two colors

6 With color A (shown as pea green), make a chain with a multiple of 3. **Row 1**: Dc in sixth ch from hook, dc in next ch, * ch 1, skip 1 ch, dc in next 2 ch *; repeat from * to * across, ending ch 1, skip 1 ch, dc in last ch. Fasten off.

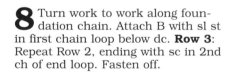

7 Attach color B (turquoise) with sl st in next to last ch of beginning chain. **Row 2**: Ch 1, sc over chain below, ch 3, work 2 dc over same chain below, * work (sc, ch 3, 2 dc) over next ch-1 arch *; repeat from * to * across, ending with sc in last dc. Fasten off.

8 Turn work to work along foundation chain. Attach B with sl st in first chain loop below dc. **Row 3**: Repeat Row 2, ending with sc in 2nd ch of end loop. Fasten off.

9 Attach B to first A dc and ch 1. Holding yarn under center of strip, * insert hook in open space between dc and make a chain (free ch), insert hook between next 2 dc and work chain, enclosing dc (attached ch).

10 Insert hook just after next dc and make another attached dc *; repeat from * to * across. Sample shows completed trimming.

Raised Stitches

These raised stitches, worked around post of stitch below, are like the one used for ribbings (see page 1). You can make crossed stitches, cables, and other richly textured patterns. Master the technique and invent your our patterns!

Cables

1 Make a chain with multiple of 7, plus 6. **Row 1 (right-side row)**: Hdc in third ch from hook and in each remaining ch. Ch 1, turn. **Row 2 and all wrong-side rows**: Sc in each stitch across. Ch 2, turn. **Row 3**: * Work hdc in 4 sc, work post dc as follows: yo, insert hook right to left under post of hdc below next sc, draw up loop, (yo and draw through 2 loops) twice to complete dc.

3 **Row 5**: * Hdc in 4 sc, skip first post dc, and work post dc on second post dc.

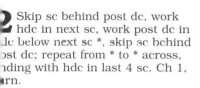

2 Skip sc behind post dc, work hdc in next sc, work post dc in dc below next sc *, skip sc behind post dc; repeat from * to * across, ending with hdc in last 4 sc. Ch 1, turn.

4 Ch 1, now work post dc around the skipped post dc (crossover made), skip the 3 sc behind crossover *; repeat from * to * across, ending with hdc in last 4 sc.

5 **Row 7**: * Hdc in 4 sc, work post dc in post dc below next sc (always skip sc behind each post dc), hdc in next sc, post dc in post dc below next sc *.

Raised Stitches

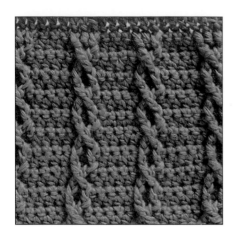

6 Repeat from * to *, ending with hdc in last 4 sc. Ch 1, turn. Repeat Rows 2 through 7 for pattern. Sample shows completed pattern.

Lattice

7 Make chain with multiple of 4, plus 3. **Row 1 (right-side row):** Hdc in third ch from hook and in each remaining ch. Ch 1, turn. Do not count turning chains as stitches. **Row 2 and all wrong-side rows:** Sc in each hdc across. Ch 2, turn. **Row 3:** * Hdc in sc, skip 2 sc, work a post treble (tr) around hdc below next sc (to make post tr: yo twice, insert hook right to left to draw up loop, yo to work off loops 2 at a time).

8 Ch 1, reach back with hook to work post tr around hdc below first of 2 skipped sc (crossover made), skip the 3 sc behind crossover, *; repeat from * to * across, ending with hdc in last 2 sc. Ch 1, turn.

10 Repeat from * to *, ending hdc in last 2 sc. Ch 1, turn. **Row 7:** Hdc in first sc, skip 2 hdc, work post tr around first post tr of next crossover, ch 1, work post tr over first of 2 skipped hdc, skip 3 sc behind crossover, hdc in next sc, then repeat from * to * on Row 6, ending hdc in last 2 sc. Work in pattern as for Rows 4 through 7, keeping continuity of diagonal lines formed by raised stitches. Sample shows completed lattice.

9 **Row 5:** Hdc in 3 sc, skip first crossover below, * on next crossover work post tr around first (underlying) post tr, ch 1, then reach back to previous crossover to work post tr over second post tr, skip 3 sc behind new crossover, hdc in next sc *.

Tricolor Raised Stitch Pattern

is stitch is also worked with post , but the effect is quite different. requires a lot of yarn, but the pattern is good for making warm winter ats.

Basic pattern

1 With color A (shown as light blue), chain an even number of ch. **Row 1 (right-side row):** Dc in fourth ch from hook and in each remaining ch. Drop yarn. Turn work and attach color B (pea green) with sl st to first dc. **Row 2:** Ch 4, * skip next dc, inserting hook right to left under post of following dc, work tr around the post (post tr made), ch 1, repeat from * to * across. Drop yarn.

2 Turn work and attach color C (purple) and ch 4. **Row 3:** Folding top of work down and out of way as shown, * work a post tr around the post of unworked color A stitch below (2 rows below).

3 Ch 1 *; repeat from * to * across. Drop yarn. Sample shows back of work.

4 Pick up A and ch 4, turn. (As you pick up colors to use, carry strand between rows loosely along edge of work.) **Row 4:** * Work post tr around post of color-B tr 2 rows below (note position of yarn to use on all wrong-side rows) ch 1 *; repeat from * to * across. Drop A.

5 With B, work (post tr around color-C tr 2 rows below, ch 1). Continue in this manner, alternating colors for each row and always working tr around the post of tr 2 rows below. Remember to draw up yarn correctly on right- and wrong-side rows. Sample shows completed work.

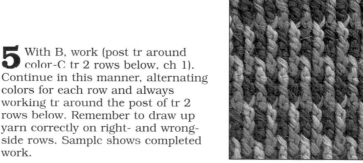

Tricolor Raised Stitch Pattern

Checkerboard

6 With color A, make a chain with multiple of 10, plus 8. **Row 1 (right-side row)**: With A, dc in fourth ch from hook and in each remaining ch. Drop A; attach B and ch 3. **Row 2**: With B, skip first dc and count ch-3 as first tr, work post tr around next 4 dc, drawing up loops as for wrong-side rows.

7 * Work post tr around next 5 dc as for right-side rows, work post dc around next 5 dc as for wrong side *; repeat from * to * across. Drop B. With C, ch 3, turn.

8 Row 3: With C, work post tr around color-B post tr, working as for right side over right-side tr (as they now face you) of previous row, and wrong side over wrong-side tr. Drop C. With A, ch 3, turn.

9 Row 4: With A, work post tr around color-C post tr, working as for right side over wrong-side tr (as they now face you) of previous row, and wrong side over right-side tr. **Row 5 and 6**: Changing colors, work as for Row 3.

10 Continue to alternate the checkerboard pattern every 3 rows and rotate colors at the end of every row. The sample shows completed checkerboard pattern.

Flower Motif to Appliqué

This flower motif requires a bit of patience to make, but that is well worth it when the flower is finished. The size of the thread or yarn used determines the size of the motif. A fine cotton thread will yield a delicate trim for collars or pockets, heavier yarns produce trims for tablecloths of curtains.

2 Ch 5, turn. **Row 2**: * Work (sc, ch 3 and sl st in third ch from hook for picot, 2 more picots, sc) over ch-4 arch between clusters, ch 1, sc in top of next cluster *; repeat from * to * twice more. Fasten off.

4 Cut long strand of green to use as base of two side leaves. Anchor strand and attach yarn from ball to center sl st of 5-sl st group of leaves, ch 1 and draw up loop from under extra strand and work sc, enclosing strand.

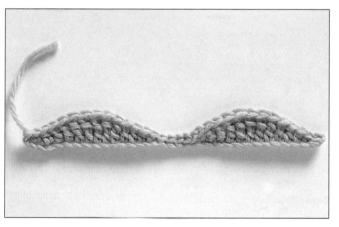

1 With yellow, ch 3. Work 9 sc in third ch from hook. Join with sl st to first sc to form flower center. Fasten off. **Row 1**: Attach orange to first sc; ch 4 (counts as first tr), work (tr in same sc, 2 tr in next sc), retaining last loop of each; yo and draw through all loops on hook (first cluster made), * ch 4, work 2 tr in each of next 2 sc, retaining last loop of each; yo and draw through all loops on hook (another cluster) *; repeat from * to * twice more. Last sc is unworked.

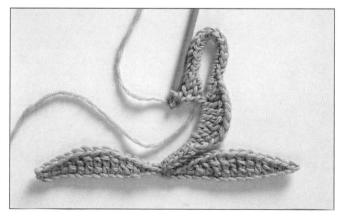

3 With green, ch 34. **Row 1**: Sl st in second ch from hook, working 1 stitch in each remaining ch across, work sc, hdc, 2 dc, 5 tr, 2 dc, hdc, sc, 5 sl st, sc, hdc, 2 dc, 5 tr, 2 dc, hdc, sc, sl st. Fasten off.

5 Continue working over strand, working 5 sc, hdc, 2 dc, 5 tr, 2 dc, hdc, 15 sc, hdc, 2 dc, fold leaf over (as shown), and work tr by inserting hook between dc and tr on other section of leaf to join.

Flower Motif to Appliqué

6 Work 3 more tr, working only over strand; work next tr by inserting hook between tr and dc on other side, then work 2 dc, hdc, 4 sc only over strand. Now d in third sl st where yarn was attached.

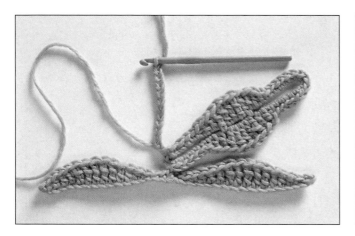

7 Without working on loose strand, ch 12 for stem.

8 Join with sl st in unworked yellow sc of flower.

9 Work sl st in each ch back to bottom of stem.

10 Now work over loose strand, working 4 sc, hdc, 2 dc, 5 tr, 15 sc, hdc; fold down top of leaf, work tr joining between dc and tr on other section, work 3 more tr only over strand, work tr joining between tr and dc, then on only strand, work 2 dc, hdc, 6 sc, sl st in same sl st where yarn was attached. Fasten off.

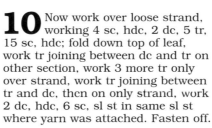

Circles Transformed into Squares

Motifs that started as circles can be transformed into squares by working longer loops or taller stitches at the four points that will become the corners. The square motif can then be easily joined in strips or larger units. The weight of the yarn used determines how delicate the motif will be.

he square rose

In a yarn ring (see page 18), ch 4. **Rnd 1**: Work tr in ring.

2 Continue to add tr until you have 23 for a total of 24, counting the ch-4 as the first tr. Join with sl st to top of ch-4.

3 **Rnd 2**: Ch 5 (first tr and ch), * work tr in next tr, ch 1 *.

Repeat from * to * around. Join with sl st to fourth ch of ch-5. **d 3**: Sl st in next ch (last ch of -5), ch 1, sc over ch-1 where sl st s just worked, work (ch 3, sc over xt ch-1) five times, ch 6 for corner, * work (sc over next ch-1, ch 3) e times, sc over next ch-1, ch 6 *; peat from * to * twice more. Sl st first sc to join.

5 **Rnd 4**: Sl st in first ch of first ch-3 arch, ch 5 (first tr), work 3 more tr, retaining last loop of each on hook; yo and draw through all loops on hook (first cluster made), * ch 3, work 4 tr over next arch, retaining last loop of each; yo and draw through all loops (another 4-tr cluster) *; repeat from * to * three more times. ** Ch 3, work (2 tr, ch 3, 2 tr) over corner ch-6, ch 3, work (cluster, ch 3) over each arch to next corner **; repeat from ** to ** twice more, ch 3, work last corner, ch 3. Join with sl st in top of first cluster.

Circles Transformed into Squares

6 **Rnd 5**: Sl st in first ch of next arch, work first cluster as for last rnd, work (ch 3, 4-tr cluster) three times, * ch 4, work (5 tr, ch 5, 5 tr) over corner ch-3 arch, ch 4, work (4-tr cluster, ch 3) three times, work 4-tr cluster *; repeat from * to * until fourth corner is completed, then ch 4, join to top of first cluster. **Rnd 6**: Sl st in first ch of next arch, work first cluster, * work (ch 3, 4-tr cluster) twice more, ch 5.

The orange square

8 Work as for previous square until Rnd 2 is completed. **Rnd 3**: Sl st in next ch, ch 1 and sc over first ch-1, ch 3, * sc over next ch-1, ch 3 *; repeat from * to *. Join with sl st to first sc. **Rnd 4**: Sl st in next ch, ch 7, work (dc over next ch-3 arch, ch 4) four times, * work (tr, ch 4, tr) over next arch for corner, work (ch 4, dc over next arch) five times, ch 4 *; repeat from * to * until fourth corner is completed, ch 4, join with sl st in third ch of ch-7.

7 At corner, work (tr, ch 1) in each of 4 tr, tr in last tr of 5-tr group, ch 5, work (2 tr, ch 3, 2 tr) over corner ch-5, ch 5, work (tr, ch 1) four times in each of 4 tr, tr in last tr of 5-tr group, ch 5 (corner made), skip ch-5, work 4-tr cluster *; repeat from * to * until fourth corner is completed, then ch 5, join to top of first cluster. **Rnd 7**: Sl st in first ch of next arch, work first cluster, ch 3,* work 4-tr cluster, ch 5, at corner work (sc over next ch-1 between tr, ch 3) three times, sc over ch-1 between last 2 tr, ch 5, sc over next ch-5 arch, ch 5, sc over ch-3 arch, ch 5, sc over next ch-5 arch, ch 5, work (sc over next ch-1 between tr, ch 3) three times, sc over ch-1 between last 2 tr, ch 5 (corner made), work 4-tr cluster, ch 3 *; repeat from * to * until fourth corner is completed, then ch 5, join to top of first cluster. **Rnd 8**: Sl st in first ch of next arch, work first cluster, * ch 5, sc over next ch-5 arch, ch 5, work (sc over next ch-3 arch, ch 3) twice, sc over next arch, ch 5, sc over next ch-5 arch, work (ch 6, work 2 tr over next arch) twice, work (ch 5, sc over next arch) twice, work (ch 3, sc over next arch) twice, ch 5, sc over next arch, ch 5, work 4-tr cluster *; repeat from * to * around ending last repeat with ch 5, sl st in top of first cluster. Fasten off.

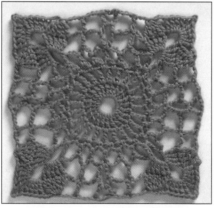

9 **Rnd 5**: Sl in next 2 ch, ch 8, * skip 1 dc, work (tr, ch 4, tr) in next dc, ch 4, skip 1 arch, tr over next arch, ch 4, at corner work (5 tr, ch 5, 5 tr) over ch-4 arch, ch 4, skip 1 arch, work tr over next arch, ch 4 *; repeat from * to * until fourth corner is completed, ch 4, join with sl st to fourth ch of ch-8.

10 **Rnd 6**: Ch 7, * skip arch, (tr, ch 3, tr) over next arch, ch 3, tr in tr, ch 3, tr in 5 tr, retaining last loop; yo and draw through (cluster), (5 tr, ch 3, 5 tr) over ch-5, cluster on 5 tr, ch 3, tr in tr, ch 3 *; repeat from * to * through fourth corner, ch 3, join to fourth ch of ch-7. Fasten off.

Circular Insert

Motifs can be joined in this method to make a circular insert for a table-cloth center, collars, or neckline trims. Make the flowers first, then join them with crocheted rows at inner and outer edges.

1 Ch 9 and join to first ch with a sl st to form a ring. **Rnd 1**: Ch 3, dc, * ch 4, work tr and dc, retaining last loop of each; yo and draw through all loops on hook *.

3 Rnd 2: * Sc over next ch-4 arch, ch 7, wrap yarn four times around hook...

2 Repeat from * to * seven more times, ch 4. Join to top of dc.

4 ...work treble treble (tr tr), retaining last loop on hook; work 3 more tr tr, retaining last loop of each (5 loops on hook)...

5 ...yo and draw through all loops, ch 7, sc over same arch (petal made) *.

Circular Insert

7 Make the desired number of flowers. Join them as follows:
Outer edge: Attach yarn to top joining stitch on any petal, ch 3, dc in top of same petal, * ch 9, sc in top of next petal, work joined tr and dc (as for Rnd 1) in next petal.

6 Repeat from * to * eight more times. Join with sl st to first sc. Fasten off.

8 Yarn over hook six times, inser[t] hook into top of next petal to work *quintuplet* treble (work off 2 loops at a time as usual).

9 Ch 9, yo six times, insert hook into same petal just used, then into top of any petal on next flower, and draw up loop and complete another quintuplet treble (qtr); work joined tr and dc in top of next petal on new flower *.

Repeat from * to * for outer edge, joining last flower to first with qtr, then sl st in dc at start of edge. Fasten off.

10 **Inner edge**: Between qtr joining (of outer edge) and the inner edge leave 1 petal free and attach yarn to top of next petal on inner edge. Work ch 3, dc i[n] same petal, * ch 9, work joined tr and dc (as for Rnd 1) next petal, work qtr in next petal, ch 9, work another qt[r] in same place and join next flower in the first petal after outer-edge joining, ch 9, work joined tr and dc in next petal on new flower *; repeat from * to * around inner edge, joining last flower to first as before. Fasten off.

Rounded Borders

These borders work well for lightly ruffled hems as well as for round pieces of fabric. The first border is worked sideways so you can make it as long as you wish. The other piece is worked lengthwise on a foundation chain with a predetermined number of stitches.

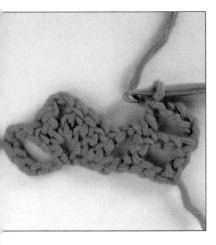

Rounded border worked sideways

1 Make a chain with multiple of 17. **Row 1**: Work (2 dc, ch 2, 2 dc) in ninth ch from hook, dc in next 2 ch, work (ch 2, skip 2 ch, dc in next ch) twice. Ch 5, turn. **Row 2**: Dc in next dc.

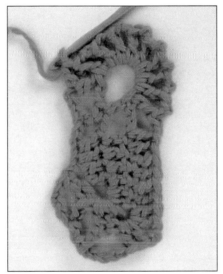

2 Ch 2, work dc in next 4 dc, work (2 dc, ch 2, 2 dc) over next ch 2 arch, ch 2, skip 2 dc, dc over turning ch. Ch 5, turn. **Row 3**: Skip first arch, work (2 dc, ch 2, 2 dc) over next arch, dc in next 6 dc, ch 2, dc in next dc.

3 Work (ch 2, dc) eight times over ch-5 arch, dc on end ch of foundation ch below.

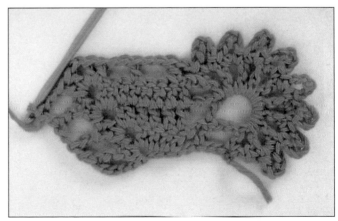

4 Ch 1, turn. **Row 4**: Work (sc, ch 5, sc) over each ch-2 arch just made.

5 Ch 2, dc in first dc of 8-dc group, ch 2, skip next 3 dc, dc in next dc, ch 2, skip 3 dc, work (2 dc, ch 2, 2 dc) over ch-2 arch, ch 2, dc in center ch of ch-5 arch.

Rounded Borders

6 Ch 5, turn. **Row 5**: Skip first arch, work (2 dc, ch 2, 2 dc) over next arch, dc in next 2 dc, work (ch 2, dc in next dc) twice. Ch 5, turn. Repeat Rows 2 through 5 for pattern. Sample shows completed border.

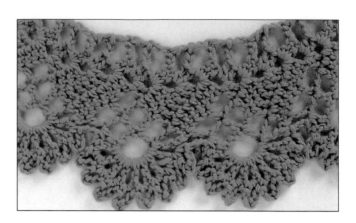

Rounded border worked lengthwise

7 Make chain with multiple of 8, plus 3. **Row 1**: Sc in second ch from hook and in each remaining ch. Ch 5, turn. **Row 2**: Skip first sc, dc in next sc, * ch 2, skip 1 sc, dc in next sc *; repeat from * to * across. Ch 3, turn. **Row 3**: Work (dc, ch 2) in each arch across, ending dc over last arch, dc in third ch of same arch. Ch 5, turn. **Row 4**: Repeat Row 3, but ending dc over last arch, ch 2, dc in top of ch-3. Ch 1, turn. **Row 5**: Sc in first dc, * sc over next arch, ch 5, sc over next arch, sc in next dc, ch 11, work tr in eighth ch from hook, tr in next 3 ch.

8 Sc in next dc below, sc over next arch, ch 5 *; repeat from * to * across, ending with sc over next arch, sc in third ch of ch-5. Ch 5, turn.

9 **Row 6**: * Work ch 3, sc in third ch from hook for picot, ch 2, sc in arch below, ch 2, work (3 dc, picot, 3 dc, picot, 3 dc, picot, 3 dc) over ch-7 arch.

10 Ch 2, sc over arch below, ch 2 *; repeat from * to *, ending with picot and tr in last sc. **Row 7**: Sc in first picot, * sc in next picot, ch 5 *; repeat from * to * across, ending sc in next to last picot, then sc in last picot. Fasten off. Sample shows completed border.

Interlocking Rings

This elaborate border is actually easier to work than it looks. The border can be used for curtains and bedspreads as well as for belts and straps.

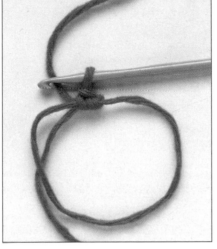

1 With color A (shown here as purple) make a yarn ring (see page 18). Draw up a loop and work 30 sc in ring.

2 Join with a sl st in first sc. Pull yarn end to tighten ring into a perfect circle.

3 Ch 2 and work an hdc in each sc. Join with sl st to top of ch-2. Fasten off.

4 With color B (shown as orange), make a yarn ring through the color A circle as shown with yarn coming under rim to center and passing out over rim. Work a row of 30 sc, rotating yarn ring as needed to work stitches.

5 Complete first sc row and work hdc row as before (steps 2 and 3, above).

Interlocking Rings

6 Fasten off B. With A, make yarn ring through circle just finished, with yarn over rim to center and passing out under rim, and work sc row as before.

7 Complete circle with an hdc row as before. Fasten off. Continue alternating colors and interlocking yarn ring with previous circle as shown for each color as you add circles until you have reached the desired length. Arrange the circles as shown and pin them together to hold them flat and in place for working the border edges.

8 Attach B to upper edge. **Row 1**: Sc in each of 4 hdc at center top of first ring, * make joining by inserting hook into next hdc, then into underlying hdc of next circle and draw up loop; yo to complete joining sc, sc in next 4 sc at top of this new circle *; repeat from * to * across. Ch 1, turn.

9 **Row 2**: Sc in each sc across. Fasten off. Turn work. Attach A to first sc. **Row 3**: Sc in first 3 sc, * work ch 3, sc in third ch from hook for picot, sc in next 3 sc *; repeat from * to * across. Fasten off.

10 Rotate work and crochet these 3 rows of edging on other side of border. Sample shows complete border.

Patchwork from Scraps

You can use up scraps of yarn following these designs and the granny square on page 101. Use the same type of yarn on any one project. If you are using many colors of scraps, use only one color for the borders to keep the piece unified.

Three-color square

1 With color A (white), make yarn ring (page 18). **Row 1**: Ch 3, work 2 dc in ring, ch 2, work (3 dc, ch 2) three times in ring. Join with sl st in top of ch 3. Fasten off; attach color B (red) to ch-3. **Row 2**: With B, insert hook in space between ch-3 and next dc and ch 4, dc in space between next 2 dc, work (ch 1, dc) 3 times over ch-2 arch (corner), work (ch 1, dc in space between next 2 dc) twice *; repeat from * to * twice more, work corner, ch 1. Join to third ch of ch-4. Fasten off.

2 Attach color C (green) to center dc at any corner. **Row 3**: * Sc in center dc, ch 3, sc in next dc, ch 3, skip next dc, sc over ch-1 between next 2 dc, ch 3, sc in first dc at corner, ch 3. *

3 Repeat from * to *, ending with sl st in first sc. Fasten off.

5 Next strip: Join the first square to the end square on strip, working joining as before. For the second square, join on 2 sides. Work Row 3 on the 2 outer (free) sides, ending with sc in first dc at corner, ch 3. Then work joining as in step 4, ending at next corner with sc in first sc at corner, ch 3. One side is joined.

4 Make a second square, work until 3 sides of last row are completed, ending with sc in first dc at corner, ch 3. **Joining**: Sc in center dc at corner, ch 3, sc in next dc, ch 1, sc in corresponding arch of previous square, ch 1, skip 1 dc on new square, sc over ch-1 between 2 dc, ch 1, sc in corresponding arch of previous square, ch 1, sc in first sc at corner of new square, ch 3. Join with sl st to first sc. Fasten off. Joining is made on 2 center loops along side. Make a strip of joined squares, then begin the second strip.

Patchwork from Scraps

6 Now repeat joining as in step 4 to join next edge. Join with sl st to first sc to complete.

7 You can fill in the large openings at the corners to make the piece more stable. Attach A to a free ch-3 arch in the opening and ch 3, then retaining the last loop of each stitch, work a tr over each free arch around the opening (8 loops on hook).

8 Yo and draw through all loops on hook. Fasten off. Fill in all the openings where four squares come together.

Four-color variation

9 Work as for previous 3-color square until Row 2 is done, working with yellow, then pink. **Row 3**: Attach C (green) to center dc at any corner. Ch 1, work (sc, ch 1, sc) in first dc, then sc over each arch and in each stitch, working (sc, ch 1, sc) in center dc at corners. Sl st in first sc.

10 Row 4: Attach D (purple) to a corner ch-1. Ch 1, sc over ch-1, * ch 3 skip 2 sts, sc in next st *; repeat from * to * around, ending ch 3, sl in first sc (4 arches on each side). Fasten off. Work second square until Row 4 is worked along 3 sides. Continue Row 4, joining as follows: * ch 1, sc in corresponding arch of first square, ch 1, skip 2 sts, sc in next st *; repeat from * to * across last side. Sl st to first sc. Join all adjacent sides in this way as you add squares. Sample shows completed unit.

Index